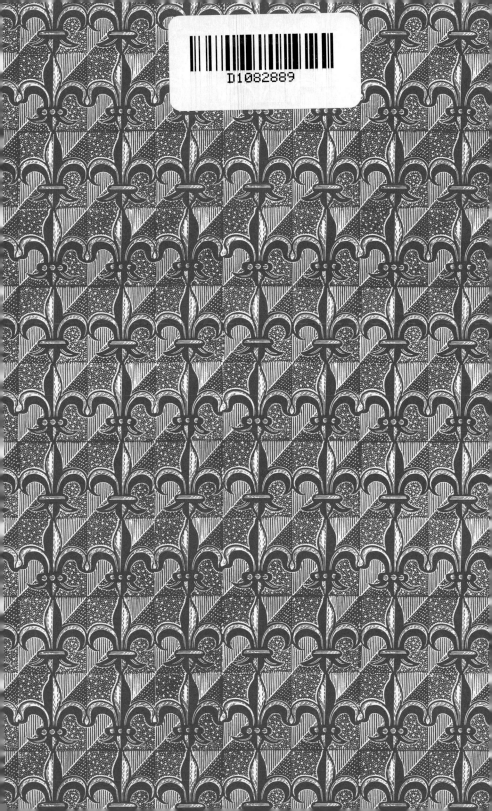

BEST FRIENDS

Rachel and David Cecil as they were when I
made their acquaintance

Leslie Hartley

Cynthia Asquith

Rachel and David Cecil in later life

BEST FRIENDS

Memories of
RACHEL and DAVID CECIL
CYNTHIA ASQUITH
L. P. HARTLEY
and some others

BY

JULIAN FANE

SINCLAIR-STEVENSON
and
ST GEORGE'S PRESS

SINCLAIR-STEVENSON

First published in Great Britain by
Sinclair-Stevenson Limited and St George's Press
7/8 Kendrick Mews
London sw7 3hg, England

British Library Cataloguing in Publication Data
Fane, Julian, *1927–*
Best Friends: Memories of Rachel and David Cecil, Cynthia
Asquith, L. P. Hartley, and some others.
1. Britain. Social life, 1901 – Biographies – collections
I. Title
941.0820922

isbn 1-85619-005-6

Typeset by Rowland Phototypesetting Limited, Bury St Edmunds, Suffolk
Printed and bound in Great Britain by Clays Limited, Bungay, Suffolk

TO

JONATHAN, HUGH and LAURA

CONTENTS

INTRODUCTIONS

L ONG AGO, IN that dawn of time when I was seventeen years old, my parents received a letter from a friend who was giving a dance in London for her two daughters. The writer was the Duchess of Devonshire, and the particular point of the letter was to ask if I would like to come to the dance.

My potential hostess and her daughters were not known to me. But my parents spoke of the Duchess with affection and admiration, and urged me to say yes. They hardly needed to: I was all for fun and a jaunt to London, eager to meet new people, and imagined I was about to make my mark in the great wide world beyond the confines of Gloucestershire.

The year must have been 1943. It was wartime: my brother was already a soldier and I would be joining the army in a few months. And relations and friends had been and were being killed and wounded in the fighting. Yet I cannot claim that I regarded the Devonshires' dance rather as if it had been the Duchess of Richmond's ball before the Battle of Waterloo. On the contrary, I recall with astonishment my blindness to the burning issues of the day. I suppose I was in the happy trance of youth, exclusively self-centred or at any rate short-sighted.

I

The scene of revelry was to be 23 Knightsbridge, a Georgian terrace house near Hyde Park Corner which was rented out for what are now called functions: it was demolished after the war. I stayed the night with my aunt, my mother's sister, who lived in a sunless ground floor flat in a mansion block at the unfashionable end of Edgware Road. At the appointed hour I braved the blackout and the bombs to get to the dance, wearing my blue suit and best shirt: dress was informal at such social gatherings during the war – anyway I had no proper evening clothes.

Although still grateful for that invitation, I cannot say I enjoyed myself much. My only memory of the evening is of a tongue-tied quarter of an hour with the Devonshires' younger daughter, Anne Cavendish, roughly my contemporary and perhaps as shy as I was. I remember dancing with and speaking to no one else – but I scarcely spoke to Anne; and the next day I shook the dust of the metropolis from my feet, and was doubtless relieved to resume my rustic pursuits.

Time passed, and I was again on the receiving end of the hospitality of the Devonshire family. The army had ordained that I should continue my military training at a camp in the wilds of Derbyshire. The season was winter and the weather cruel, and my comrades in arms and I were living in tin huts. Cold was the order of the day – and the night. Endeavouring to be less cold was our chief preoccupation. And entertainment was provided by nothing but the parades at dawn presided over by Regimental Sergeant Major Brittain. RSM Brittain was a Guardsman, tall and portly – the size of his thighs did not allow the heels of his highly polished boots to touch when he stood to attention – with a voice said to carry for eight miles and a talent to instruct, dominate and terrify large concourses of rebellious soldiery. He was kind and gentle in his private life, and always dignified; but his public personality was that of a fire-eating martinet, and he carried discipline to the positively theatrical lengths of having anyone who displeased him, even Warrant Officers, marched off in close arrest.

During my six-week sojourn in this camp, I received a note from Elizabeth Cavendish, Anne's elder sister, telling me her home was adjacent and that she would ferry me there for lunch on a certain Sunday, unless she heard in the meanwhile that I was otherwise engaged – perhaps my mother had informed Elizabeth's of my whereabouts.

Accordingly, on the relevant Sunday, I waited by the camp Guardroom and gate, was duly picked up and ferried to Churchdale Hall.

Elizabeth was easy to get on with, and remains so. She introduced me to her father, a smallish wiry man with an outsize moustache, and to another guest, staying for the weekend, an elderly American lady, Mrs Corrigan by name. The house was unassuming, but wonderfully warm and luxurious in comparison with my army quarters.

Soon a butler announced lunch, and the Duchess joined us in the dining-room in rather a rush. I see her clearly across the gulf of forty-odd years – she made an indelible impression. She was middle-aged, in her later forties, and all that I then expected a mother to be, that is to say she kept her distance and caused no embarrassment. At the same time her beauty, charm and humour, and especially

3

some ethereal romantic quality, quite bowled me over. She apologised for her lateness. She spoke well of my parents. She encouraged me to air my views, for instance of military training and what was wrong with it. She laughed at my worst jokes. Her distinction had nothing to do with smartness or fashion. She wore comfortable clothes, a tweed skirt and twin-set maybe, but managed to look elegant with pretty rings on her long white fingers and her rows of pearls, strung individualistically – small pearl, knot, larger pearl, knot, small pearl again, and so on.

At that first of the many meals I have been pleased to eat at the dining-room tables of members of the Cavendish and Cecil families – the Duchess of Devonshire was born Lady Mary Cecil, sister of my future friend David – conversation was jolly and stimulating, also surprisingly general: the rule about children and young people being seen and not heard seemed not to apply.

It emerged that an expedition had been planned for the afternoon. I agreed to drive the Devonshires' car, an ancient Austin, and the Duchess, Elizabeth and Mrs Corrigan, over to Haddon Hall, another ducal property, belonging at the time to the Duke of Rutland.

On lichened flagstones in the courtyard of Haddon, as I remember, Mrs Corrigan slipped and fell and hurt her wrist: in fact, although nobody knew it until later on, she had broken her wrist. She was uncomplaining beyond the call of social etiquette.

Laura Corrigan had been the target of much criticism and ridicule in palmier pre-war days. She was very rich, and in England, and probably in the USA too, had entertained on a lavish scale. Stories circulated of bran-tubs at parties, containing Cartier jewels for her guests. Needless to say, only a tiny minority of those who accepted her largesse were truly thankful for it.

The Devonshires' interest in her would never have been materialistic: setting aside their integrity, what could she have given them that they did not already possess? They must have liked her, and were loyally having her to stay in her older age.

I INHERITED AN awkward digestion from my father. After a year of military victuals I was suspected of having a duodenal ulcer and invalided out of the army. The war ended, I was soon well again, and felt lucky – the more so when I received another invitation from the Devonshire family. I was asked to spend the weekend at their summer residence, Compton Place in Eastbourne.

For most of us, there is an uniquely charmed time of life between doing what our parents and the state want us to do, and doing whatever we discover and agree has to be done, our job or career, our means of earning a living. It is when we please ourselves, and usually and sadly is characterised by its brevity. We are free as never before and perhaps afterwards, and may be happier.

I was nineteen, and unintentionally as aimless as any Zen Buddhist becomes by long years of study and endeavour. I liked writing, but had not yet recognised any vocation to write, and would not have dared to think of ever being a professional writer: I was rather the wax tablet waiting to be written on. I scarcely knew who I was, let alone what. I was ready for everything and nothing – nothing except romance and present laughter.

I caught a train at Victoria Station, recall sunlight on the South Downs from Lewes onwards, arrived at Eastbourne and then at Compton Place – and a season of enchantment began for me.

Compton Place is within walking distance of the centre of Eastbourne and the sea-front. At the end of a hundred-yard drive, the grey stucco-faced house squats behind a gravel circle and is – or was – flanked by evergreens.

I can only describe it as it used to be. The modesty of the facade of the building, suggestive of a small Georgian manor or big vicarage, was deceptive: for the house was roughly square, and part of it may have been hidden behind those laurels and yews. There were five so-called reception rooms on the ground floor, drawing-room, library, dining-room, billiard-room and sitting-hall, where tea was sometimes served, also various offices, one or two staircases, and a wide passage running from the front door to the garden door at the back; and above, on the upper floor, innumerable more or less large bed-rooms.

The decorative style of the interior was shabbily grand. Rooms seemed not to have been done up for centuries; but comfort that is pretty and cosy is usually the result of unremitting attention and effort. Although the archi-tectural proportions, and the fine plasterwork and the quality of furniture and pictures, were to some extent lost

6

on me, they must have underpinned my conviction that the house was perfect.

Ozone mingled with the aroma of high-class country living, scents of pot plants and cut flowers and pot-pourri, redolence of log fires and tobacco smoke, especially the smoke of the flat Turkish cigarettes – or were they Cypriot? – smoked by the Duke. And the proximity of the ocean gratified the sense of sight. Light reflected skywards from the surface of the waters, and back again, was lighter. Accustomed as I was to the moist veil drawn across the face of the western side of the country, I noticed with pleasure the clear coastal brightness of this south-eastern corner.

The Compton Place garden consisted of a few beds of roses behind the house, and a grass tennis court on one side. Beyond, mown lawn sloped up to and was crowned by woods of forest trees. This view was short, enclosed, but strangely secretive and satisfying. A distant flint wall, visible between tree trunks, sheltered the kitchen gardens.

But bricks and mortar, the location and the furnishing of a house, do not necessarily create a happy atmosphere within it.

And two facts of social life at Compton Place might have had a negative effect on visitors. The weekend parties were a mixed bag of young and old, relations, close friends and strangers, rich and poor, beauty and wit, plain Janes and dull dogs: theoretical homogeneity was neither aimed at nor achieved – entertaining on a generous scale cannot be confined to a clique. Secondly, the food served, although always delicious, seemed to youthful appetites to be in shortish supply, perhaps inevitably since rationing was still in force, and even if ration books were handed in on arrival; while drink did not flow as it would in similar circumstances in these more alcoholic days. A permanent drinks tray disfigured no room. A glass of sherry was sometimes on offer before dinner. A toper had to make do with excellent claret with meals and port after them.

Yet I feel sure I am not alone in having so enjoyed visits to Compton Place in that sunny post-war summer.

Elizabeth and Anne's younger group usually amounted to half a dozen of us. We ate strawberries and gooseberries in the kitchen garden – within minutes of clocking in for my first visit I was eating those strawberries: they seemed to be in a class of their own. Through a door in the far wall of the kitchen garden we would meander into the town, perhaps to call on the Devonshires' friend and ultimately their dependent, the antique dealer Miss Locking, or to listen to the brass band on the promenade under its band-stand with turquoise-coloured dome. We laughed as it were twice over at certain jokes: for instance at holiday makers with peeling noses and knotted handkerchiefs on their heads, and at ourselves for joining in the fun, licking ice-cream cones and searching for seaside postcards. Occasionally we giggled through a set on the tennis court or a game of billiard fives; and we lazed on long chairs in the sunshine with the Sunday papers; and, still more excitingly, played French and English, also called Flags, by moonlight.

I occupied a bachelor room with tapestries covering the walls. In the morning Edward, the butler Edward Waterhouse, would burst in to draw the curtains and collect the clothes I had worn on the previous day, ostensibly to valet them. I had met him at Churchdale Hall. He was overweight, bald, pale-complexioned, good-natured and humorous, and might have stepped straight out of P. G. Wodehouse. He was too rushed to stop and talk before breakfast. He would just bundle up one's dinner suit and shoes and pound along to the next gent's bedroom. Incidentally, far from ironing our suits, Edward must have put them through the mangle, and somehow he rendered our shoes dirtier than they had been.

He had entered into service with the Devonshire family long ago, perhaps as Boots or Pantry Boy, and he eventually died in it. I believe the same applied to the other three members of the staff I knew, the cook Mrs Weaver, the Duchess's maid Winnie Woodman, and the chauffeur Lewis James. All were expert at their jobs, and would not have spent their whole lives working for the same employers if they had not been happy to do so. No doubt their happiness, their contentment, contributed to the agreeable atmosphere in the Devonshires' houses.

Miss Bolton was always the first down to breakfast. She had been Elizabeth and Anne's governess, and stayed put after they had grown up, and dedicated her existence to helping the Duke with the crossword puzzle. She was half-Swiss, fresh-faced, slightly eccentric and extremely fond of food. She would help herself liberally from the dishes on the methylated spirit hot-plate on the sideboard, and to coffee and cream, and the day's polite conversation, as soon as she had someone to talk to, began.

The subjective statement that Compton Place was

perfection may not convey much. Objectivity would differentiate it from other homes I had visited, and have visited since then, in one essential respect. Conversation took precedence over all possible activities. It was polite in the ancient and modern meanings of that word: civilised and tolerant, based upon mutual respect and goodwill, neither vapid nor adversarial; also well-mannered and discreet. It prolonged breakfast into the middle of the morning, and continued, except when we were changing for dinner or playing pencil games or charades after it, until bedtime. And as practised with precocious virtuosity by Elizabeth and Anne, it helped to unify the diversity of their guests.

Yet the Duke was a quiet man. He had private interests and accomplishments, apart from his public responsibilities and commitments without number. He knew a lot about wild flowers, for instance; and he spoke good French, and had a lathe for turning wood installed in a back room, and was a thoroughgoing forester in every sense. He was not only a dendrologist, and owner and planter of trees, he worked long hours in the woodlands of Compton Place, where daytime conversations were wont to be punctuated by the regular sounds of his axe.

Fine-featured beneath his moustache, slight of build with large capable hands, he was a generous and benevolent host and seemed to enjoy his chatty home-life. He would throw an apt word or pertinent anecdote into the pool, and he unexpectedly shone at charades. But his nature was shyly reserved and taciturn.

The talkativeness, the readiness to discuss almost

everything and reason it out, the wish and the will to entertain verbally, and to encourage others to give tongue spontaneously and naturally, without ever showing off – all this derived from the Duchess and had long been the tradition in her family, the Cecils of Hatfield House.

That the Duke and Duchess should have created so much fun for me and many others while mourning their elder son Billy, who had been killed in the war, was signally unselfish and deserving of gratitude; and their surviving children are by no means excluded from my belated tribute.

The Duchess had adopted Billy's dog, a giant poodle called Bimbo, and the Duke kept a snapshot of Billy in the lid of his Russian silver cigarette box.

BILLY'S WIDOW SOMETIMES stayed at Compton Place. She was born Kathleen Kennedy, nicknamed Kick, and was the elder sister of Jack, later President of the USA, and of Bobby, Teddy and the rest of the ill-starred Kennedy clan. She was a very nice and attractive young woman in the American style, energetic and sporting, and much loved by the Devonshire family.

Kick was older than me. But the conversational connections between everyone at Compton Place also bridged the gaps between generations and nationalities.

The oldest visitor I remember was Lord Quickswood, the Duchess of Devonshire's uncle. Although only about eighty years of age in the later nineteen-forties, he seemed ante-diluvian, and perhaps not just because I was young and innocent.

He was the seventh and last child of the third Marquess of Salisbury, who was the second Robert Cecil to serve a British Queen as Prime Minister: he served Queen Victoria, his forebear Queen Elizabeth I. Lord Quickswood was another illustrious flower of that most remarkable of family trees. As Lord Hugh Cecil he had been a Member of Parliament, a politician of great promise and a noted orator. But he objected to the legislative proposal to allow a man, a widower, to marry the sister of his deceased wife – he regarded it as an invitation to murder; and he retired from politics altogether when the vote went against him. Later he became the Provost of Eton College, despite his conviction that boys should be educated by the chaplain at home, and he remained in this post throughout the Second World War.

He had a pleasing appearance, bald but broad-browed, solid yet refined; was a confirmed bachelor, monk-like and other-worldly; and wore tweed breeches or knickerbockers and stockings with his matching jacket and waistcoat and his stick-up shirt-collar. He had been thirty-two when Queen Victoria died in 1901. His nickname was Linky: could it have been a reference to the Missing Link?

He was witty as well as quirky. An acquaintance was said to have paused in the middle of some long-winded recital to ask him: 'Am I boring you?' – to which he replied: 'Not yet.' He preached a sermon about death in Eton College Chapel and warned the boys that eternal torment was almost certain for most of them, but a very few might hope for merciful annihilation. He thought it was unnecessarily fussy to build air-raid shelters, at least for Etonians, when war broke out.

I remember the Duchess, his niece, offering him more sandwiches or cake at teatime, and his oracular refusal: 'I have made my tea.' In between meals, he repaired to his bedroom.

A visitor even more regularly at Compton Place than myself was Lord Quickswood's contemporary Sir Edward Marsh, Eddie Marsh, sometime Private Secretary to Winston Churchill, friend of Rupert Brooke and patron of poets and artists, who bought so many young painters' pictures that he ran out of walls to hang them on and then had them fixed to the ceilings of his house in London.

I understand that the Devonshires allowed him to store some of his chattels in their country house or houses at the beginning of the war, and Eddie paid visits to these chattels thereafter, for weekends and holidays, whenever he felt like it. He too was a bachelor, but he had a mincing manner and sported a monocle, and his worshipful attitude to Rupert Brooke, dead for thirty years, provoked covert satire. Amongst his better quips was his description of Sir Clive Bossom as neither one thing nor the other.

Once Lady Cunard came to stay. The Devonshires had known her for a long time, since before she changed her Christian name to Emerald, and they still called her Maud. She was old, tiny, much made up, birdlike: a parakeet or budgerigar. She entertained non-stop in her suite at the Dorchester Hotel. But her art as hostess differed from that of the Duchess: it was forceful and provocative, it sought the clash of opinion, it wanted

13

conversational feathers to fly, and it attracted representatives of café society or today's glitterati.

At Compton Place she declared that she could not believe in the Bible because the events it described happened so long ago.

I was shocked in my prim jejune way by this squib, the more so because it was tossed into a Christian household, and I reacted against Lady Cunard's social brittleness and sensationalism. But the Devonshires took her in their stride. And in time I heard on good authority that she was something of a split personality, a dependable friend, a devotee of books and music, and a vulnerable woman in private, saddened beyond repair by the loss of the love of Sir Thomas Beecham.

Lady Cunard may have been in a minority at Compton Place in that she was related to neither the Duke nor the Duchess. Many guests, if not most, had some link with the Cavendish or Cecil families, which are just about equally old and reproductive: I did, although it was not discovered for several years. Whether or not the Duke liked his relations, he surely took the rough with the smooth of the convention of primogeniture: I mean he recognised that the dukedom and the lion's share of the Devonshire inheritance imposed upon him the obligation to provide a centre for, basically food and shelter for, anybody with a drop of his blood in their veins, or allied to such a person.

Genealogy is for me a closed book – or perhaps I ought to say a good reason to close a book. Suffice it therefore to say that I arrived at Compton Place one evening, a Friday evening as usual, it must have been, and found the company assembled in the library, where two men were standing in front of the low wood fire and talking: they were the Duchess's younger brother David Cecil, and their cousin Arthur Gore, later the Earl of Arran.

Not the least of David's lucky breaks was to get through life without one of the adhesive pet-names that his family went in for. The oldest member of his generation of Cecils, Beatrice, who became Lady Harlech, was Mima to her intimates – why, nobody seems to know. His elder brother, another Robert Cecil, the politician Lord Cranborne and future Marquess of Salisbury, a great man of infinite dignity, was Bobbety. The Duchess of Devonshire's Christian name Mary turned into Moucher. And Arthur Gore was saddled with Boofy.

Those names suggestive of empty-headed frivolity were misleading; and Bobbety's was doubtless a ball and chain to drag through his career. The best thing about them, or the only good thing, was that they amounted to a sort of testimonial to unworldliness.

Boofy Gore, who might have been nominated for membership of the Drones Club, was in fact an energetic and successful journalist on the *Daily Mail*, and a hard worker for charity. He was fortyish, very clever and amusing, and wore spectacles and had prematurely grey hair.

David, roughly the same age, was extraordinary. The better I knew him, the more out of the ordinary I realised he was; but I refer above to his external characteristics, which took a little getting used to. He almost chain-smoked with almost manic enthusiasm, holding his cigarettes in strange ways, for instance between his third and little fingers. He gestured with large hands attached to

15

pale wrists, flapping one or other of them to indicate the momentary frustration of not being able to find the right word. And his voice rose and fell as if beyond his control, now hitting a boyish high note, now deep and gravelly. He spoke in such a rush that he sometimes spluttered, and he cackled with unmelodious laughter.

Of course I had heard of him both as writer and social star; though I think I had read none of his books at this stage. The fame of *The Young Melbourne* had reached my ears; the Cavendish girls often mentioned their uncle with affection; and a candid female photographer from America, whom I met somewhere, had said to me, 'There's only one face worth photographing in your country, and that's Lord David Cecil's.'

He must have had a romantic, if somewhat overbred, countenance when he was young: he was sketched, painted, sculpted – but then many of his friends were painters. To me, at first, he looked like a poet who had strayed into a boxing ring. His nose was not flattened, but it seemed to have been tweaked out of its natural shape, and his front teeth were in trouble. At the same time his complexion seemed to emit a pallid gleam, perhaps owing to the gemlike interior flame of his dedication to art. His brow was metaphorically high, but physically rectangular and jutting – nothing weak about it; and his heavy iron-grey hair grew or was brushed straight across the top of his head from one ear to the other.

He may not have had the regular features of his sister Moucher, or the reposeful solidity of his uncle Linky; his appearance was nonetheless as distinguished as theirs, he would and he did stand out from any crowd, and his vitality, his liveliness, was a quality all his own, and indeed exceptional.

He and Boofy in the library at Compton Place carried my conversational education a stage further. They were so funny, nimble-witted, inexhaustible. Their talk was light-hearted, yet reinforced by general knowledge and by erudition. Above all, it had that ingredient of pleasure which the influential young turks of today – or was it yesterday? – frown upon and call insincerity: to wit, charm.

At dinner, probably on that same evening, I sat next to Rachel Cecil, David's wife, who told me she played the recorder. I liked her and was struck by her youthfulness, but can recall not much else about our meeting.

After dinner on one of the evenings of our weekend together, after port and pencil games, David was prevailed upon to read aloud from his work in progress, *Lord M.*, the sequel to *The Young Melbourne*, dealing with Lord Melbourne's later life, Prime Ministership and death.

He read well, despite the speed of his delivery and occasional inaudibility. His voice was the more impressive for its unconventional inflections, and never failed to express the sense of what he was reading. The passage he treated us to was the description of Lord Melbourne's first visit to the house of Mrs Norton, Caroline Norton, with whom he soon fell in love. It included this sentence, which I have always remembered: 'He was ushered up into a minute drawing-room, bright with flowers and muslin curtains and almost filled by a large blue sofa, from which rose to greet him a young woman of glittering beauty – all opulent shoulder and raven's wing hair, who bending forward a little, looked up at him meltingly from under sweeping lashes and whose blood, as she spoke, mantled delicately under a clear olive skin.'

The book, so far as it went, was in typescript. Typing is an inexact science, as everybody dependent on the typewritten word has reason to agree. At some later date David told me that a typist's draft of the complete book contained a classic error. He said a sentence that should have run: 'Lord Melbourne ended his days in tranquil obscurity,' was typed thus: 'Lord Melbourne ended his days in tranquil obscenity.'

Two more memories of Compton Place remain with me. Princess Elizabeth, now Queen Elizabeth II, and Princess Margaret were invited to stay, and the poodle Bimbo had a field day, chasing and biting all the police-men on guard and hiding behind trees in the grounds. And on another occasion we made a great bonfire of the branches of a tree the Duke had felled, and kept it going late into the night.

Bonfires are autumnal. Summer's short lease was over; life drew me in other directions; I did not return to Compton Place in the meanwhile, or see David and Rachel again for a few years.

MAKING FRIENDS

KNOCKING ABOUT BEFORE I became a writer included a brief spell as an undergraduate at Cambridge. My decision to go there was really indecisive: my aim was less to study and gain a careerist qualification than to keep my parents quiet and convince them I was not an idler and wastrel.

In the course of my sojourn at Cambridge I was asked by yet another Robert Cecil, today's 6th Marquess of Salisbury, to lunch at Hatfield House. I had made Robert's acquaintance in boyhood, then I got to know his wife Mollie, and they must have wished, amongst other things, to give me the pleasure of meeting his grandparents and to show me over the ancestral – and their own eventual – home.

Genealogy barges in for all my resolutions to keep it out. With apologies, I have to explain that my host at the luncheon in question, my friend Robert's grandfather, was the 4th Marquess, a very old gentleman, born in 1861, son of the Prime Minister, brother of Linky, and father of Mima, Bobbety, Moucher and David – he had been a front-rank politician in his heyday; while my hostess Lady Salisbury was the aunt of Boofy Gore.

The size of Hatfield, and its long royal and politically

powerful history, were daunting. It must have been used as a hospital or for some public-spirited purpose during the war, and was now largely shut up. I remember a sitting-room and a dining-room on the first floor occupied by the Salisburys, and in between them another grand high-ceilinged room with a wood-turning lathe standing deep in shavings and sawdust. The Duke of Devonshire had probably copied his father-in-law in having just such a lathe at Compton Place; but in my experience the Duke only worked his to crack nuts.

Lord Salisbury had been a notably handsome young man, and he merited every complimentary epithet descriptive of old age. His hair was silvery white, his papery complexion fresh, his eye clear and mild, his manner gentle and courteous. His looks were even more refined, and his bearing more monk-like, than Lord Quickswood's: he was the image of a sainted sage in a stained glass window or a Dutch picture. He was perhaps excessively religious. David would say with regret and sympathy that his father, chaste bachelor, faithful husband, fond parent, who had devoted his whole life to good causes, was tortured latterly by the grievousness of his sins.

Lady Salisbury wore her long hair piled on top of her head, was as jolly as her spouse was unassertively melancholy, and her ready laughter was a surprising cackle, like David's.

At lunch my nervousness proved to be superfluous to requirements. I saw how the daughter of the house, Moucher Devonshire, had come by her inheritance of human warmth, enthusiasm and lack of affectation. In time to come, when I read the works of Tolstoy, I associated his palatial Russian houses and superannuated Russian nobles with the Hatfield of that visit and its gracious lady and especially its pious lord. Tolstoy seems to have had earthier passions than old Lord Salisbury; yet he understood, conveyed fictional impressions, and finally shared the tendency of aristocracy to relate ever more closely and humbly with what might be called its only superior, the Lord Almighty, and increasingly to disdain the things of this world, the worthwhile majority of which it already possesses.

A side-effect of my introduction to the Salisburys was that I received a letter in a shaky hand from Lady Desborough, Lady Salisbury's lifelong friend, asking me over to Panshanger. I did not go. Perhaps I was unable to go. But I am still disappointed that I failed to avail myself of the opportunity.

Si jeunesse savait, si vieillesse pouvait!

I was ignorant of the fact that Ettie Desborough was the daughter of my great-great-uncle and namesake, the poet Julian Fane, and the mother of another poet, Julian Grenfell, whom I admire. Now I would take trouble, cancel plans, travel far, reorganise my priorities, in order to meet her, if I could. I would dearly love to discuss with her our shared ancestry; and that company of scintillating Victorian kindred spirits, the Souls, of which she and other relations of mine were original members; and the Corrupt Coterie, the clique composed largely of the children of the Souls, including her own; and her three marvellous boys, Julian and Billy and Ivo, gilded and crowned with academic success, as brawny as they were brainy, who were all killed in the 1914 war. Through

21

bereavements, through the bitterest sorrow, Ettie Desborough impressed her contemporaries by proclaiming and preaching her 'stubborn gospel of joy'. Moreover she was the first critic of David Cecil's writing. He submitted his literary effusions to her when he was at school, and said that her encouragement helped him to become a writer.

But I missed my chance of receiving similar help, and listening to and learning from Lady Desborough. And I left Cambridge, where I had wasted my time and my parents' money by scribbling stories instead of studying Beowulf, and in due course, in the traditional garret in London, wondered if I ever could write professionally. I began to work hard at last, and educate myself as best I could, and steer clear of my friends in order to do so, and serve the term of my apprenticeship.

In the middle of it Anne Cavendish got engaged to Michael Tree and invited me to their wedding, which was to be celebrated in the chapel at Chatsworth. I was also, even more kindly, invited to stay the night in the house. It had not been lived in by the Devonshire family since long before the war – I think it had been regarded as the most elephantine of white elephants. But its official wartime tenants had departed, and now it was going to be opened up for the occasion.

The weather was cold, if not particularly so by the standards of Derbyshire, and the central heating was either not working or did not extend along miles of passages into farther-flung bachelor bedrooms. The chill musty interior, and the antique lighting system rendered dimmer by missing and defunct electric bulbs, accentuated the brilliant grandeur of the rooms with roaring fires in which the party congregated and feasted in the evening before the nuptials; and the history and the size of the Duke's home – his main one – reminded me of Hatfield.

David and Rachel were there, but I do not remember talking to them much. Anne and Michael were picturesquely and quietly wed on the following day, and I returned to my labours.

THEN, IN RETROSPECT, too many people who meant more or less to me seem to have died within a short space of time. My own father died aged fifty-five, and his exact contemporary the Duke of Devonshire, who had been chopping wood at Compton Place, came indoors and sat down in the staircase hall and told Miss Bolton he was not feeling well and instantly expired.

The Lord Salisbury who had interrupted his religious meditations and woodwork to entertain me to lunch, and his brother Lord Quickswood, died. A few years later Lady Salisbury with her rollicking laugh, who said one must learn to laugh at nothing because there was often nothing to laugh at, followed suit. Thus Moucher lost her husband, and she and David their father and mother and uncle, not to mention their great family friend Ettie Desborough, in quick succession.

Eddie Marsh died a lonely death, also Emerald Cunard, mourned and missed by her intimate friends.

And fate, like some malign conjuror, always has a card up its sleeve. Kick Hartington, Kick Kennedy that was, Billy's widow beloved by the Devonshire family, was killed in a flying accident.

Meanwhile my aim to win fame and fortune was taking a little longer to achieve than optimism had expected. In other words my years of age and obscurity were mounting up.

I had been trying in vain to write plays. At least I never quite persuaded the powers-that-be to put one of my plays on a stage. Later, David Cecil expressed the view that it was a mistake for most aspiring writers to try to write for the theatre, films or TV. He said that too many people had to be in on the presentation of such entertainment – there were too many decisions to be taken and logistical difficulties, and above all too much money involved; and playwrights seemed to need experience of acting and perhaps the happy-go-lucky thespian temperament to boot. He believed literary inclination stood a better chance with a book.

Whether that is so today, as big business lords it over most publishing houses, is a moot point. Unmitigated capitalism is unlikely to improve the prospects for first books, and will certainly lower those superior artistic standards that do not make money, or enough of it. On the other hand, who wants collectivist control of art?

But maybe every old and new obstacle put in the path of artists does toughen and refine talent, as well as reducing the number of contenders for the prizes that time alone can bestow.

I was not so philosophical in my play-writing days.

The only service time performed for me was to remind me it was passing. I worked harder, I tried harder than writers should, and as a result of forcing the pace I got stuck and found myself in the desert wastes of uncompleted enterprise and unfulfilled hopes.

That I had started to write on a shoestring, with insufficient funds at my disposal, therefore without the blessing of parties interested in my welfare, did not help me to keep calm, be patient, exude confidence and reassure everyone.

At last, when I was twenty-four or so, I felt I had reached the end of my theatrical tether, and should desist from struggling with plays that I might not be able to finish and nobody would perform, and possibly stop writing altogether.

What changed things was a chance remark. I was staying in the country, spending the weekend in our family home, and, to be precise, scything some rough grass, when a female friend of advanced years, who had been having tea with my mother, came and complimented me on my handiwork and said: 'You're lucky to have been brought up here – you'll always have your happy childhood.' She was definitely not dropping an oblique literary hint. Yet she was no doubt aware of my problems, although I trust I never complained of having set myself to solve them, and wished to console me if she could.

Anyway, my inner response was immediately to think: 'Yes, I have my childhood – which is not the plot of a play or a fabrication – but real and true – and I shall transfer it on to paper, write it all down, without the fear of not being able to or the worry of having to decide what ought to happen next.'

And almost there and then I began *Morning*, following in the footsteps of many other writers who had to go back in order to go forward.

Prose suited me better than dramatic dialogue. I felt as much at home with the medium as with the subject matter, and discovered I could mix invention with experience, and still reflect that I was simply telling the truth. I took nothing for granted, and dared not think my luck had changed. But it was a heady time for me, in which, according to the paradoxical metaphor applied to writers, I found my voice.

At some stage I broke off to visit Anne Tree. A cousin of Michael Tree's had died in sad circumstances, Michael had inherited his house in Kent, and he and Anne lived there. The house was Mereworth Castle, actually not a castle but the famous copy of the Palladian villa La Rotonda, hauntingly beautiful, intricately constructed, for instance the smoke from every fire in the house issues from a single chimney in the centre of the domed roof, and indubitably a nightmare to maintain.

At Mereworth – pronounced Merryworth – Anne and I traced our family connection. A relation of mine had built it, he had been inspired by seeing La Rotonda on his Grand Tour of Europe, he set the work in train in his early twenties, and he had a carved stone frieze added to the exterior of the pair of pavilions and perhaps of the house as well: the frieze consists of his crest, the bull's head emerging from a coronet, and that of his wife, the coiled serpent of the Cavendishes. Mereworth has a chequered and curiously ominous history. The first and by no means the last of its chapter of accidents was that my ancestor and Anne's can hardly have moved in before they had to sell it and move out.

Anne had given a home to her old governess Miss Bolton. Following the death of the Duke of Devonshire, the Dowager Duchess, Moucher, decided to spend her widowhood in London, where Elizabeth lived; and the new and present Duke, Andrew, was unable to afford to keep Compton Place going and so was forced to let it. From these upheavals Miss Bolton had to be protected. She had grown accustomed to comfortable irresponsible life in the bosom of the Cavendish family, an approximate continuation of which Anne and Michael could and did offer at Mereworth. She occupied a flat in one of the pavilions and joined the Trees and their guests for at any rate lunch and tea – I remember her clapping her hands when tea was served. Perhaps she had breakfast too – the fullest English sort; but she returned to her own quarters for dinner.

Throughout that weekend she was much in evidence as usual, a stolid presence dozing over the crossword puzzle, rousing herself only to scold Anne with fond ineffectuality or consume a heavy meal or toddle home. She might have seemed to be the more in evidence because the David Cecils were staying, and her occasional observations, meteorological as a rule, or whimsical in the Swiss style, were such a contrast to David's quicksilver conversation and Rachel's empathy and responsiveness.

We had the nicest possible time, or I did, and on the Sunday afternoon in the Long Gallery, the double

27

drawing-room with painted ceiling and two great fire-places, questions relating to my occupation were put to me by Rachel.

Authors, even aspiring ones, soon learn the costly lesson that the more they talk about their writing the less they write. Lots of authors, though apparently not David, also find that the more they talk about anything what-soever the less they write.

But Rachel's questioning was different. It was not only that she was so gentle, diffident, genuine, serious; she was almost a professional, being married to David – I was as yet unaware of her own literary breeding and background.

I therefore broke what was going to be the habit of a lifetime and told her I was writing a book about childhood and offered and promised to send her a chapter.

My confidence in her was not – never was – misplaced.

Almost by return of post she wrote back: 'You can't think with what excitement and interest I read the beginning of your novel.'

These words were the first of the approximately thirty thousand of her side of our correspondence.

RACHEL PROVED HER 'professionalism' to me, that is to say her cognisance of the susceptibilities of author-ship, by reacting with the minimum of delay, and in writing, to my typescript. 'Amateurishness' has driven many an author half-mad by its belated acknowledgment of work submitted, by its lukewarm or uncertain reactions, if any, by not giving reasons for whatever it thinks and feels, and by not putting such thoughts and feelings on paper, where they can be scrutinised at leisure and in detail. Bad publishers and lazy literary agents twist authors' tails in the same way and without the excuse of ignorance.

Rachel had innate expertise in these matters, for she was the child of the marriage of authors, her mother Mary MacCarthy who wrote *A Nineteenth Century Childhood* and *A Pier and a Band*, and her father the high-class critic Desmond MacCarthy. Moreover, especially by virtue of the latter, whose fabled charm and intelligence seem to have made him welcome in every set, clique and class, she had been a junior associate of the members of the Bloomsbury Group. She was often interrogated by Virginia Woolf, and referred to the intoxicating effect of her curiosity and humorous comments. But I think Rachel – or am I thinking of a thought of David's? – considered Bloomsbury as a whole rather pretentious and sexually confused and ridiculous.

Her attitude to the writing of her friends was softened by perfect manners and the kindness of her heart. Yet she never lowered her literary standards or compromised her values – although perhaps I should not say so, since luckily for me she approved of most of my work.

Her approval of the chapter of *Morning* was a landmark in my life: it was the first good opinion of the first bit of my first book by an outsider, an objective reader and qualified judge.

It was also one of the increasing number of signs of the growing general sympathy between herself and her husband and me.

The upshot of our triangular communications about *Morning* was that the Cecils asked me to stay the weekend at their home in Oxford.

David was then in his early fifties, Rachel in her later forties. She still looked like a girl – she never lost her slight, trim, girlish figure. While most of her gestures reinforced the youthful impression, her walk, which was brisk and decisive, gave away the secret of her maturity. She had neat brown hair, again done in an uncomplicated young – or maybe old-fashioned – style. Her face was oval, her high eyebrows created a slightly surprised expression, her complexion was pink and white and pure, and her teeth were a trifle too long rather than too short. Her clothes were pretty and sensible, conventional and unobtrusive. She could be compared, quite descriptively, to a bird, a mouse, a Jane Austen heroine, even to Jane Austen herself. She was clever enough to hide her cleverness or not to parade it, and, despite appearances, hard-headed and infinitely sophisticated. She spoke with a sort of hum in her voice and articulated her words crisply. Her smile was easy and sweet, and her laughter ever ready. The form of her wonderful sense of humour was not so much to make jokes as to see the funny side of everything.

She and David and their three children, Jonathan born in 1939, Hugh in 1941, and Laura in 1947, lived in a neo-Queen Anne house in Linton Road in those veritable groves of academe of North Oxford. It was detached, stood in a sizeable garden by urban standards, and was located in a large so-called estate of similar, if smaller, houses, probably built in the thirties. The area was quiet and pleasant, intricately divided up by close-boarded fences, shrubby and shaded by ornamental trees, mainly what John Betjeman called 'bypass cherries', and inhabited by a preponderance of dons and professors and their families.

The word pleasant again applies to the architecture of the Cecils' house outside and in, faintly praising though it may be. I remember an adequate hall with a steep staircase, a light sash-windowed sitting-room of extended rectangular shape, and a dining-room also longer than it was broad.

The sitting-room was painted blue. Its undistinguished proportions and gas fire contrasted oddly with the pretty decoration, curtains, covers and so on, and the pictures and furniture, some of which surely bore the grand Hatfield stamp. A Chinese screen zigzagged between the door and one of the armchairs on either side of the fire. There was a French marquetry desk in the far corner, reserved for Rachel's use.

I have no recollection of a study for David at Linton Road. Could it be that he wrote in his room at New College? But Linton Road was bigger than it seemed. The three children and a young nanny fitted into the second or attic floor, and a resident cook was accommodated somewhere.

The Cecils' bedroom, and bedrooms for guests, two of them, I guess, were on the first floor. Rachel's decorative art was to conceal art: in all her homes, the bedrooms that I slept in were strikingly simple, models of unluxurious and unfussy cosiness. Beds were comfortable; otherwise equipment was basic, except for a Victorian portrait of a Cecil forbear in a gilded frame, for example, and for books. Bookshelves wall-mounted or free-standing or fitted, and brimful, bursting at the seams, found their way into every room. And last thing at night David was inclined to produce half a dozen extra volumes for the guest to read before going to sleep.

The starting-point of the winding academic path that led the Cecils to 7 Linton Road was David's mother's insistence that he should have a job, or the qualification to get one, as well as a vocation to write. His native caution assented, although in later life he wondered – like most writers – if he should have devoted more time to literary composition.

In 1928, aged twenty-six, he became a Fellow of Wadham College. But the following year he published his first book *The Stricken Deer*, a biography of the poet Cowper, which was a success; and in 1932 he retired from teaching, married and went to live with Rachel in the village of Rockbourne.

One of the many attractions of Rockbourne, at least for David, was its proximity to Cranborne Manor in Dorset, that second stately house given to his Elizabethan ancestor Robert Cecil by a grateful monarch, where his parents had dwelt before inheriting the Salisbury title and Hatfield House, and he and his brother and sisters had spent an idyllic childhood.

In the next six years he wrote *The Young Melbourne* and *Hardy the Novelist*. Then in 1938 he was offered a Fellowship of New College, and considered it an opportunity not to be missed. Besides, if Jonathan was already on the way, he might have feared the financial pinch; and if the worst came to the worst and war was declared, he would need a more obviously useful occupation than writing books – he was not fit to fight, he had had tuberculosis when young, and he was too clumsy and absentminded for practical tasks. He returned to Oxford.

Neither 7 Linton Road, nor his previous home at Rockbourne, housed David in the style to which he was accustomed by birth and upbringing. Cranborne Manor, made of mellowest stone and pale local stucco, a fairy-tale castle in a sylvan setting with the village church in its garden, is not so magnificent as Hatfield, but still a big place. Admittedly David's mother had spartan notions of comfort, or, to put it another way, did not deign to notice or bother about discomfort, and I understand that, while she was in charge at Cranborne, visiting bachelors would sleep – if they could sleep – on straw palliasses; nevertheless, she doubtless depended on an Edwardian army of staff to feed her family and friends, service a score of bedrooms, mow vast lawns and cultivate acres of walled kitchen garden.

David never complained of drawing the shorter straw in the game of chance in which the firstborn male child scoops the pool. He was mercifully immune from the common affliction of people in his position: the younger son complex. Far from fretting over the fact that he was not the Marquess of Salisbury, nor the owner of great estates, nor rich enough to have no common or garden money worries, he thanked his lucky stars publicly and sincerely that the awesome responsibilities borne by his

33

elder brother, then by his elder brother's son, were not his. He was in favour of the unwritten rule of primogeniture widely observed in this country not only because it freed him to do as he pleased and become what he wanted to be; but also because, in the particular case of the Cecils, any division of the family spoils between the children of the house would have necessitated the disposal and dispersal of assets and records, a national treasure-trove of the history of four centuries of life at the top of social and especially political trees. From another point of view he was sorry to think that in a sense his brother and then his nephew, and indeed their wives, were the prisoners and slaves of their inheritance.

If David ever rebelled against his family, as children will and artists have to inasmuch as they must de-class themselves, he had done so long before I got to know him better. He deeply loved and had been loved by his mother, honoured his father, was very fond of his siblings and endlessly interested in his other relations, who, after all and in general, were endlessly interesting people. And he was extraordinarily objective in respect of the accident of his birth; he was endowed with that cool objectivity for which his ancestors were renowned; he judged everyone, dukes, lords and ladies, dons, undergraduates and dust-men, by the same standards. He was not snobbish, even if, strange to relate, he preferred congenial and amusing company and decent behaviour and civilised surroundings.

He really belonged to the classless, or anti-class, guild of artists. Yet a fascinating, subtle, scarcely definable aura of aristocracy, of pedigree, of the grace of privilege, always clung to him. He could not help being a proper gentleman: he was above meanness and pettiness.

His *Portrait of Jane Austen* contains sentences applicable to himself in this sociological context.

'Jane Austen,' he wrote, 'talks of class distinctions blithely and frankly and without any of the uneasy embarrassment that afflicts most subsequent English novelists when they tackle this distressing subject. This came from the unconscious confidence engendered in her by her own secure social position . . . It was also due to the fact that she lived in an age when class was taken for granted by herself and everyone she knew as a right and natural feature of any human society.'

STAYING THE WEEKEND with David and Rachel was a conversational marathon, or a banquet of talk. In thank-you letters I would say my brain was sprained and I was getting over verbal indigestion: I was not used to talking so much. David was an exception to the rule according to which outstanding talkers become monologuists – he conversed with you or tried to, he drew you out, and you had to try to keep up with him. And Rachel's passionate interest in everything was irresistibly stimulating.

Talk seemed not to tire them: they both had vitality and quite a lot of energy, and they were in training, so to speak. It started early in the morning. Neither Linton

Road nor the Cecils' future homes were large, and not the least of the peculiarities of David's voice was that it carried through brick walls. A guest was lulled to sleep by sounds of animated chat emanating from their bedroom, and woken by their carrying on from where they had left off the night before. David's dramatically high and then low notes, the rapid fire of his exposition of some theory, of observation or recollection, and his sudden cackling laugh, alternated with the equable twitter and hum of Rachel's contributions.

Breakfast at nine was 'cooked'. Although Rachel hated housekeeping, and developed a phobia of cooking when she had to do it later on, she organised ample simple and delicious fare for her guests. We usually had eggs and bacon on Saturdays, and invariably chipolata sausages on Sundays, followed by toast she herself made in a toaster, and coffee in big cups.

Geoffrey Madan describes staying with the Desboroughs at Panshanger thus: 'Day breaking hot and hard, like morning in the tropics: you find yourself sitting in tight to breakfast, in the full glare of talk, discussing immortality.'

Immortality, and any other topic for that matter, might be discussed at breakfast with the Cecils. But the talk never glared. It was nonetheless serious for not being intense. And the only fault I ever found with the days we talked through together was that they were inclined to be too exciting and exhausting.

A constitutional was customary before lunch on Saturdays. We would cover more ground at a faster pace than I expected to. David compensated for abruptly stopping, as it were to search for a word or the means of conveying an idea, by almost running to catch up; and Rachel with her slim physique seemed able to trip along for ever.

In the afternoon we usually sallied forth for a more adventurous walk or to see a sight. David donned his hat again, and perhaps threatened to drive us to our destination. He had three hats to my knowledge in the thirty-odd years of our friendship: a cross between a trilby and a porkpie, a tweed or flat cap, and a blue cap with a brim in Chekhovian eternal student style, which he pulled low down on his forehead.

He drove as he walked — not actually stopping the car to make a conversational point, but looking at his passengers, even those in the back seat, as he did so. He was either unaware of the risks he ran or impervious to danger, and with relaxed abandon crashed the gears and stepped harder on the accelerator.

Evidently Rachel did not like to show a lack of confidence in his driving, at any rate in front of outsiders, and, prior to departure, if she had not already appropriated the keys of the car, would suggest: 'Shall I drive, David?'

There was also evidence that he thought he was as competent as she was, for he would answer politely and without inhibitions: 'Of course, if you want to. But supposing I drove, you could enjoy the view.'

She had to laugh at his illusion that anyone could enjoy anything while he was at the wheel, although she was equally polite: 'Would you mind if it was the other way round?'

Sometimes he misinterpreted her diffidence and firmly fetched the car to spare her trouble and scared his passengers nearly to death on the open road, which was nowhere near open enough when he was careering along it.

But as a rule he deferred to her; and she would utter one of her jerky exclamatory unfinished sentences and an apologetic giggly laugh – 'Oh – well – yes – good!' – meaning she was sorry to have insisted on trying to save lives.

After our expedition to a National Trust house, for instance, or to some interesting village church or bluebell wood, we would disperse to our bedrooms to read, rest, sleep or just keep quiet until teatime. The Cecil children did not join us for meals at Linton Road: I think I was only asked to stay there during Jonathan and Hugh's terms at boarding school, and when Laura was still too young for social life.

On Saturday evenings one or two local friends were asked in for a drink or more likely to have dinner, and on Sunday mornings after church friendly undergraduates in residence were summoned for sherry.

The last lap of my visits was always the best for me. Towards the end of Sunday it must have become clear to David and Rachel that the high hopes of visitors had not been dashed, that the weekend party had been another smash hit, and the host and hostess could relax, desist from effort, and yield to the holiday mood: I refuse to believe that they were happier because their visitors were leaving in the morning – my own happiness in the circumstances had nothing to do with the fact that I would soon be going home.

Did David change into an old red velvet smoking jacket and downtrodden slippers for dinner? I seem to see him dressed like that, standing in front of the roasting gas fire for as long as he could bear to, partaking of a pre-prandial vermouth, smoking feverishly and talking his head off.

His mode of dressing was a mixture of the studied carelessness of the aesthetes of the twenties, when he was an undergraduate, and a reassuring tweediness. He confined his less conventional apparel to a floppy bow tie of velvet, say, or a fancy waistcoat, but he was cognisant of the farther-reaching implications of such dandyism: he was declaring his allegiance to the cause of art and beauty, asserting his individuality, and associating himself with the theories of French and English *fin de siècle* post-romanticism, which argued that your clothes were the outward sign of inward, and even absolute, truth.

We had dinner, and all talked long and late, and laughed and laughed, and mounted the stairs slowly, pausing for yet more conversation. Once again Rachel would make sure that guests' bedrooms were in order and comfortable, while David rummaged around for extra books for guests to read overnight. Eventually, regretfully, we said good night – and a sort of coda to every one of those precious days in the company of the Cecils ensued.

It consisted of the slamming of doors. I never knew exactly who did and who did not slam them, but suspect Rachel as well as David, and, in time, each of their offspring. At Linton Road, last thing at night on the Friday of my first visit, I was startled by – as I imagined and imagine – Rachel banging into the marital bedroom and David into his dressing-room; then by David banging out of his dressing-room and into the bathroom and back again; then by Rachel banging in and out of the bathroom;

then by David banging out of his dressing-room and into the bedroom, saying something to Rachel, and returning with a couple of bangs; then by one of them descending the stairs and banging the doors on the ground floor; and so on. It was amazing and amusing.

I could not, let alone would not, pick holes in the Cecils' hospitality. I have stayed in bigger houses with a larger staff serving richer food and rarer wines than theirs; but none in which more trouble was taken to make guests welcome, or where one laughed and learned more in such a sympathetic atmosphere.

The short answer to the question of how it was done is that David and Rachel were blessed with many remarkable and widely recognised gifts, intelligence, humour, sensibility, lovability.

I suppose I had a compelling additional reason to revel in their company: because it was complimentary. That a couple old enough to be my parents should single me out for friendship was flattering. Considering David's fame, and that he and Rachel were so popular and sought after, I was honoured. And the incense of their attention was even headier when I remembered, when they reminded me, that the origin of it was my writing.

My gamble, my years of secret scribbling were paying off, my application for membership of the select club of authorship was finally seconded by David Cecil, while Rachel's encouragement almost convinced me that my literary tribulations were over.

But in retrospect the happiness of knowing them, that they gave me and innumerable others, mainly derived from and was traceable to their marriage.

Matrimonial bliss can be exclusive. I have heard it said that there is nothing sadder than a happy marriage – sadder, that is, for others.

Once or perhaps twice I was present when David kissed Rachel on the cheek after some slightly protracted absence. I never saw him hold her hand, or noticed any intimate exchange between them, an ambiguous glance, a murmured aside. Some years ago a mid-Atlantic cultish dogma laid down that if you did not show how difficult it was to express yourself, hesitate, mumble corrections of every sentence, you were glib, and if you did not speak your love and prove it publicly, at least with kisses and caresses, you were a cold fish. The Cecils were neither inarticulate nor demonstrative. Psychoanalysis in one of its crazier moods might have decided that they were repressed. But the commonest sense thanks God for repressions, and entreats Him with prayers and supplications to repress the unsociable urges of a few more of His children.

David and Rachel treasured and guarded the boon of privacy. They were modest, the opposite of boastful, and showed off about nothing – certainly not about having solved that riddle of existence which is posed by music-hall comedians thus: how to be happy though married? And they were too polite to embarrass anybody if they could help it, and too kind to wish to be the cause of jealousy, envy or the aching of lonely hearts.

But they re-defined the word compatibility in spite of themselves. They were apparently incapable of quarrel-ling, arguing, displaying irritation or impatience one with the other. Neither could stop himself or herself listening to what the partner was saying, shutting up to listen with interest or to laugh. They had to be in constant communication, propinquity and harmony.

And their friends basked in the lovely warm radiance of their relationship, or this one did – and in my sanguine youth without realising its rarity.

7 LINTON ROAD

YOUNG WOULD-BE WRITERS suffer from the advice of their elders, if not their betters, since everyone thinks he or she can write, that there is nothing much to writing, given time and the opportunity to have a bash at it, and that success is guaranteed if you avoid certain booby-traps and follow his or her directions.

But the making of sentences and the telling of stories by means of them are as individualistic as handwriting itself; and for different people success equals different things, money, for instance, or fame, or notoriety, or getting something out of your system, or getting your own back, or righting a wrong, or just seeing your name in print.

At various times and by various amateurs I was advised that writers who aspire to create deathless prose end up in hospital wards with ulcers, and I must learn the tricks of my trade in journalism; that if I had not earned a living wage from writing within a year or two I was obviously no writer and should look for alternative employment; that I ought not to write a line until I had worked my passage round the world; that I ought not to publish a line until I was forty years of age; that I should devote my whole existence to writing, and, alternatively, that I should get out of my ivory tower and mix in the market-place; and, most definitely, that I should meet other writers, with whom I could discuss literature in general and my own efforts to produce some in particular.

Luckily I managed to disregard most of these instructions. But I did come across a few writers in the period before I met David and Rachel, and I made friends with C. P. Snow and then with his wife, Pamela Hansford-Johnson. At one exciting moment Charles Snow and I were persuaded that plays we had separately written would be put on by the same theatrical impresario – eventually his was.

Charles had the eggiest of bald heads. He looked like a mole – he wore thick spectacles and had short arms and small plump white hands – and was as industrious. He had been and perhaps still was an academic when I knew him, he also had an important post in the Civil Service, he was a novelist, literary critic and occasional playwright, and may already have had irons in the political fire: he became a government minister and a peer of the realm later on.

He was self-made, he rose from humble beginnings to the top of the social pile, whereas David began at the top and succeeded in staying there.

Charles had many interesting things to say on the subject of his boyhood, which he compared with that of D. H. Lawrence. The hardship of having to get scholarship after scholarship was counterbalanced by the care and cossetting of his proud family: he generalised to the effect that no boy or girl was so privileged as the clever one born of poor parents. I think it was Charles – or was it some other friend with his sort of background? – who told me that his mother walked seven miles on each of his schooldays to bring him a better meal than sandwiches or school fare.

Herculean achievements such as Charles's are admirable. But unfortunately, as a rule, or so it seems to me, they do tend to exhaust; and they inculcate the conviction that prizes can and must be won, which may mislead adults and artists.

Quite possibly David had all that vitality, and good health and a long life, because he was a delicate child and spent a lot of his youth in bed.

Anyway, certain similarities between Charles and David – being contemporaries, teaching at Oxbridge, loving books – were superficial; but the differences of their approaches to the profession of letters went deeper.

For Charles, authorship was part of his career, maybe its crowning glory, another test of intelligence, another contest of mind versus matter, and a means of proving something to someone or everyone. He was much preoccupied by success, wondered whether or not he had 'arrived' or when he would 'arrive', kept on re-positioning himself in the hierarchical list of authors dead and alive, and had half an eye on the ultimate prize of immortality. His ambition and competitiveness were so frank and straightforward as to be disarming. Work, perhaps whatever it was, and life too, he might have likened to that game of Snakes and Ladders which we all had to play, and he was determined not to lose.

David undoubtedly had his share of ambition, without which nothing gets done, or done well. But he never compared himself with other authors in my hearing, and he never referred to the success or failure in worldly terms of his own or others' books. He was uninterested in money, and consequently in the success that is measured by it. And although he had two linked careers, teaching Eng. Lit. and writing it, by no stretch of the imagination could he have launched into a third completely new one, as Charles did into politics in late middle age.

After Charles and Pamela married, they invited me to social gatherings in their first home in Bayswater, then in their spacious flat in Cromwell Road. The circle of their acquaintance that I met was exclusively bookish: authors galore, editors of book pages of newspapers and magazines, critics, publishers, agents, and hyperactive readers who might now be called groupies – and the talk was inevitably shop.

Charles was kind to everyone, younger writers included, his competitiveness notwithstanding. He was a literary version of the happy warrior, defending culture from and attacking philistinism, and he took the view that volunteers to join in the fray and the fun were welcome.

He and Pamela were enviably prolific. They wrote at desks placed side by side in their workroom in the Cromwell Road flat. As their fame spread, they were lionised and invited to establishment functions. I remember asking them how they could do it, work so hard and write so much by day, and spend so many evenings out, in full fig and often with strangers. They replied – roughly speaking – that they relaxed better at a banquet than anywhere else.

Agreed, relaxation is not the least of the problems that

authorship has to solve. Another wiser piece of advice given me during my apprenticeship was that the first lesson a writer should learn is how to stop writing – on paper or in the head – for instance by going to sleep. The Snows' method of re-creating themselves is further proof of the essential unpredictability of the literary type.

David Cecil might not have spurned the odd banquet. He was curious and by no means stand-offish. But, for him, grand occasions would have lacked the charm of novelty: he had surely had grandeur for lunch, tea and dinner throughout his youth at Hatfield House and at the Salisburys' London home, a mansion in Arlington Street, near the Ritz Hotel. And he and Rachel would have wished to ration the social side of their lives in order to have the requisite energy for work, for play in the bosom of their family and for friendship. They relaxed in private, resisting the temptation of many of the gilt-edged invitations they must have received.

In this context too their attitude differed from the Snows'; as did their friends and acquaintances, especially the writers, who were my fellow-guests for weekends at Linton Road, or dropped in for meals or drinks.

OF ALL DAVID and Rachel's friends that I got to know, the one who would probably have felt most at ease at Charles and Pamela's parties was the novelist Joyce Cary.

Joyce's girl's Christian name was misleading: he was

thoroughly masculine. He was Anglo-Irish, a widower in his fifties when I met him, balding and handsome, looking like a dreamy hawk or, according to David, a gentleman jockey. He was the Cecils' neighbour, he lived in Oxford, mostly alone now, for his children were grown-up and had left home, and he used to come to Linton Road for an hour or two between tea and dinner, wearing his nice uniform of grey flannels, tweed jacket and black polo-necked sweater. He was also included in the Cecils' annual jaunt to see the plays at Stratford-on-Avon.

They loved him for the goodness of his heart, and were intrigued by his gentle eccentricity. His method of writing a book has been described elsewhere, but it was so unusual that the story may bear repetition. As I understand and heard David and indeed Joyce himself explaining it, he wrote innumerable character sketches and laid them out on the floor; then wrote the sort of episodes in which some of those characters might be involved; then played his kind of Patience with the various pieces of paper on the floor; and when he had piled up enough characters capable of interacting, and enough episodes that could illustrate their interaction, he would begin to write the linking passages and decide on his subject and theme and tell the tale. In real life he was as polite as he was zanily rude and violent in print.

Joyce had been an officer in the Colonial Service in Africa before he published his first book in middle age. What he had in common with Charles was a rather late literary start and unbounded enthusiasm for the vocation, profession, career, trade, practice and history of literature. Another connection between them was that they both achieved great success, and their books have suffered posthumous eclipse.

Joyce's inclination to discuss art as well as craft would have gone down better at dinner with the Snows than it did with the Cecils: David disagreed with his fervent and airy generalisations, and Rachel smiled at them with sceptical affection.

He died prematurely, heroically, characteristically in fact, and much to their sorrow.

For other friends of theirs who were writers, at least as professional as Joyce Cary and Charles Snow, and for that matter as successful, writing seemed to be a private preserve, trespassers upon which might be prosecuted. They would, if they could, keep work and play separate. Perhaps their work meant so much to them that they were reluctant even to mix with, or hand it over to, people who merely read or published it. They certainly preferred not to gossip about such a serious business, and were too canny to be lured into the maze of definitions of art.

David really came into this category, despite his temperamental approachability and his training as a teacher. But I used to be relentlessly curious about every manifestation of the literary life. Looking back, I see the unselfishness and generosity of the attention he paid to my intrusive queries and theories, and how encouraging it was that he never drew the hint of an odious comparison between my innocence and his experience.

Once or twice Isaiah Berlin came to Linton Road while I was there. He must have been in his later thirties at the time, he was a great friend of the Cecils, and I realised that he and David were in a conversational class of their own.

Isaiah still talks beautifully at record-breaking speed. I hope that hours and hours of his eloquence have been recorded for broadcasting one fine day, and for the sake of posterity. But I do not have much confidence in the relevant media, which missed a golden opportunity in the case of David, and seem to reserve their favour for the tongue-tied trivia or verbal diarrhoea of show-business.

David used to say that the early days of his friendship with Isaiah, when they were both young dons, were uniquely intellectually thrilling. He could not get over Isaiah's erudition and good humour, and above all his readiness – eagerness – to chat late into the night or the morning without flagging. The Cecils surely owed some of their enthusiasm for pre-revolutionary Russian litera- ture to Isaiah: who translated it – but too little of it – better than anyone else. At their meetings at which I was present, David and Isaiah's exchanges relating to books reminded me of a sort of expert tick-tack. David might ask: 'Have you seen such-and-such a book, what's it like, worth reading, worth buying?' to which the alternative answers were: 'Yes – curate's egg – not funny – but knowledgeable – and not a waste of money,' or: 'No – third-rate – don't bother.'

I never heard Isaiah refer to any aspect of his own work. He preferred to analyse persons, dissect personality, and poke inimitable fun at social phenomena. Sadly I have to agree that the best conversation is the one of which hardly a word can be recollected afterwards. He spoke of some wife bearing her husband six children 'in the fruitful Vale of Evesham', and he made unmalicious mock of the female dons with liberal opinions who had been giving evidence for the defence in the recent prosecution for obscenity of *Lady Chatterley's Lover*. There was considerable amusement in Oxford when these respectable ladies vowed in the witness box that D. H. Lawrence's vocabulary was not obscene, that they themselves had constant recourse to it, and that the nation was suffering greatly from not being allowed to read such a seminal and instructive study of the libido in action. The spirited contribution to the legal proceedings of Dame Helen Gardner, Editor of the 1972 edition of the *Oxford Book of English Verse*, earned her the nickname 'Four-letter Nell'.

Incidentally, the amusement over the trial of *Lady Chatterley's Lover* was not confined to Oxford. Some rustic peer spoke in the House of Lords in favour of the continued censorship of the book. A fellow-peer suggested that His Lordship was naturally worried about it falling into the hands of his daughter and the effect it might have on her. The other retorted that he was much more worried about it falling into the hands of his gamekeeper.

Isaiah Berlin had invented a sort of IQ test of his own, according to which somebody's intelligence could be measured by the number of 'mental events' that happened to him or to her in a specified period. By 'mental events' he meant thoughts that change the face of everything, new ideas that stir the soul or motivate the body: I trust I have interpreted his theory correctly. This descriptive rule of thumb was incorporated into the tick-tack which he and David employed: 'Not many mental events . . .

51

One mental event between the cradle and the grave . . . Worn out by having a mental event every morning after breakfast . . . A mental-event-a-year man.'

Sometimes John Betjeman called at Linton Road, and once we went to tea at his house in the country near Oxford, where the talk turned to the difficulty of doing up a parcel; but John's wife Penelope declared it was easy and, fetching brown paper and string, wrapped her biscuit-box there and then on the tea-table.

John was later to be my benefactor three times over in a professional sense, and I never shall forget my indebtedness to him, or cease to be grateful. And he was as laughably lovable in private as he became publicly, internationally, by means of his poetry and television appearances. I like to think we were friends, or very friendly acquaintances.

Yet I never knew quite how to respond to his fond and fanciful references to his teddy-bear, for instance. I was nonplussed by his whimsical streak, and often blinded by the science of his attitude to literature. Although he was responsible for hundreds of straightforward and percep-tive book reviews, he always seemed to talk about writing and writers no longer read widely, or at least by me – the 19th-century Scottish novelist John Galt, or an obscure poem to be found in an out-of-print hymnal.

David Cecil acknowledged his genius: not mere gush, but the ultimate accolade, coming from that quarter. David meant that John created a whole new world, or forced us to see the old world in a new way. He had rendered the unfashionable fashionable, Victorian archi-tecture, suburbia, and turned failure into success, a hefty

52

female tennis player into a *belle dame sans merci*. He had bathed the genteel pretentiousness of the middle class in the rosy light of nostalgic ridicule. He was the great modern exponent of the poetry of ambiguity.

John probably hid his shy sensitivity behind his tangential talk. But there was also a touch of one-upmanship in his resurrection of authors long dead and buried, in his admiration of artists no one else had ever heard of, and indeed in his revelation of the beauties of ugliness, and his opinion that good taste is ghastly. He was the champion of the overlooked and under-estimated – and not averse from making an effect with his heresies. He could be surprisingly competitive: he drove a car a bit like the roadhog in Bateman cartoons.

I believe that John never expressed an adverse opinion of another writer's work. But his laughter at the non-literary foibles of his colleagues could be as critical as it was infectious. He was a contemporary of Evelyn Waugh and once drove me to have a look at his birthplace, or the Waugh family home, in Hampstead. The point of the pilgrimage, and the joke for John, was to note the difference between the modest middle-class villa and Evelyn Waugh's assumption of the trappings of musical comedy grandeur.

Rachel had briefly worked for Evelyn Waugh as his secretary before she was married. She had liked him, and they had parted by mutual agreement and on good terms. She told me that many years later she went to tea with the Waughs in their elegant home in the west country, but for some reason she got stuck there, could not be fetched or catch the right train until the following day, had to accept their hospitable offer of a bed for the night, and was then escorted into the garden by Evelyn Waugh, who explained that the rule of his house was formal attire for dinner: he said Rachel would have to borrow a long dress from his wife.

David did not admire *Brideshead Revisited*, which, I understand with difficulty, was badly received by the critical community as a whole when it first appeared. He thought the book was bigoted, and that the picture of aristocratic life it presented was over-romanticised.

And he was too friendly and democratic to agree with Stendhal's design for living for artists, as Evelyn Waugh seems to have done: Stendhal urged artists to raise every possible barrier – space, social standing, wealth, love – between themselves and the rest of the world.

The three favours John Betjeman did me were as follows: before I knew him, he showered blessings on my first book; then he rescued me from the clutches of a destructive publisher; and he wrote what I believe was his final review of my *Gentleman's Gentleman*. He insisted on doing it, although in such poor health at the time. I take further pride in the fact that he liked to have that book read aloud to him for a last laugh.

ONCE, AT LEAST, Jonathan and Hugh Cecil were at Linton Road when I stayed the weekend. They did not participate in the social activities of the grown-ups: surely by choice – their parents would not have wished to exclude them in any way. I remember standing on the stairs and saying good night to them – they were dressed for bed in pyjamas and had bare feet – and I noted the prehensile length of Jonathan's perhaps fourteen-year-old toes.

I also remember Laura in the blue sitting-room, looking like Alice in Wonderland, lolling against the arm of her mother's chair and listening, while David and Rachel and I analysed the character of a mutual male acquaintance. We delved into his heredity and history, we blamed his appearance, searching for reasons that might explain and excuse his moral imperfections. Laura, aged five or six, volunteered her opinion and put the whole matter in a nutshell: 'He sounds foul.'

Memory is like appetite, which grows with eating. Now through the mists of time I see Laurence Whistler arriving at Linton Road with a mysterious bag in hand made of green baize. It contained the glass goblet which he was in the process of engraving exquisitely: he worked on it as he talked to us. His elder brother Rex, gifted painter and charmer killed in the war, had been another of the Cecils' great friends; while Laurence's wife Theresa, younger sister of his first deceased wife Jill Furse the actress, had been one of David's star pupils.

Amongst the legacy of paintings left by Rex Whistler is his conversation piece of David standing in front of the fire and obviously holding forth to the company assembled in the drawing-room of Edith Olivier, who was a myth in her lifetime: a spinster resident at and eventually Mayor of Wilton in Wiltshire, the author of chronicles of that locality, and a sort of provincial Egeria.

That I was not completely overwhelmed by the prestige of the people I met at Linton Road is a tribute to their unspoilt behaviour. Every visitor except me seemed to have fluttered down from the top of some tree; and every name mentioned – never dropped – to be the household variety. It was hard to find a book in the bulging bookshelves which had not been dedicated by the author, or inscribed, to David or Rachel or both.

On two or three occasions Rachel's particular friend Frances Partridge was my fellow-guest. Frances was exceptional not least in that she had not yet published any of her books. But her distinguished personal attributes suggested that she might write a good one at any moment, and she had links with the profession of literature through her late husband Ralph Partridge, with whom she had lived with Lytton Strachey at Hamspray, favourite rustic resort of the Bloomsbury Group, and home – heart's home at any rate – of the painter and diarist Dora Carrington, Ralph's previous wife.

I hope I knew and kept my place amongst all these leading lights, although they carried courtesy to risky lengths and encouraged me to air my juvenile views. They were extraordinarily humble, patient and tolerant, as I realise now, having tried for many years not to be distracted by youth's knocking on the door. Even Elizabeth Bowen, who made no secret of preferring to have nothing to do with young people, put up with me socially and took a benign interest in my work.

I often heard the Cecils speak of somebody called Elizabeth Cameron before I realised that Cameron was Elizabeth Bowen's married name. She was an international celebrity at this time, her novels were much admired and discussed, and we had several mutual acquaintances, who referred to her with esteem and affection. David regarded her earlier novels highly; and I gathered that he was an old close friend of hers, that Rachel was very fond of her, and they were excited that she had recently returned to live in Oxford.

I think Elizabeth would have been about fifty-five when I was introduced to her. My doubt may be partly due to the fact that she smoked non-stop, a hundred cigarettes a day or even more: the fingers between which she held them were stained dark brown, and her pale complexion and very flesh were similarly tinted, as if embalmed. She had a long face, bony yet expressive, grey hair which again was coloured by tobacco smoke, and that special look of stammerers, alternately direct and flinching, pained and triumphant. She was obviously strong-minded, and inclined to yield to the common temptation of women of her brilliant gallant type: she wore clothes not suited to her years and accomplishments.

A recent biography of Elizabeth by Victoria Glendinning paints a nicely flattering portrait of her. Miss Glendinning writes that she 'was probably at her handsomest in her thirties and forties, when she had enormous charm and distinction; and it is in later years that her face, softened, prompts the word "beautiful".' Miss Glendinning also writes: 'Alan [Cameron – Elizabeth's husband] put her into clothes with style: she was always thereafter "smart".'

Biographers who love their subjects are better by far than biographers who hate them. But Elizabeth is now an historical personage, and I would have to tell students of history that in the eye of this beholder she merited neither of the epithets in double inverted commas above. Her clothes had a propensity to show too much bare arm, or shoulder, or even leg; and her flesh, as I saw it, was ochre-coloured, waxy and corpse-like.

She had had problems in her life as well as acclaim: over love, over money. She had lost her husband, she had had to sell her ancestral home, Bowen's Court in Eire, to a man who added insult to injury by demolishing it, and she came back to Oxford probably in hopes of re-establishing the closeness of her friendship with David. Her bad luck was his good luck in being happily married to Rachel, in having had three children and become a busier man in the interval – or so it seemed. At the dinner at which I met Elizabeth, David happened to say that he felt guilty about not seeing enough of somebody and keeping in touch, whereupon she lashed out loudly: 'Guilt's squalid!'

Perhaps it was an objective conviction, and she was voicing a generalised critique of social humbug and morality. But it did not sound like that. And the Cecils deduced from her outburst that she identified with the somebody in question, and was angry with David for not being as friendly as he had been before he married, for disappointing her, and for pitying her and feeling guilty because he could pay her less attention than he once had and than she wished for.

They were chastened. They were saddened to think she had jumped to the wrong conclusion, and nursed a grievance and taken offence.

The counter-productive aspect of the episode was that David's cool rationality never did have time for anti-social tantrums and tempestuousness. I cannot believe that he would have set aside pleasurable engagements in order to rush to see anyone who had unjustly scolded him.

Consequently, or for whatever reason, Elizabeth left Oxford and settled finally at Hythe in Kent. David and Rachel again invited her to Linton Road. But more trouble brewed during that weekend, when I was also staying. One of Elizabeth's last novels, either *The Little Girls* or *Eva Trout*, I forget which, had just been published; and on the Sunday morning, the Cecils having gone somewhere and left the two of us alone, she announced that it was about to be reviewed or pre-viewed by the critics in a book programme on the radio, asked me to pop up to her bedroom and fetch her travelling transistor, and said we could and would listen together.

I did as I was told apprehensively, for David had read the book and considered it odd and difficult to understand. Elizabeth switched on the radio, and the critics duly expressed their opinions, which were unfavourable, and perhaps as obtuse as suggested by the author's comments: 'Oh no! . . . Quite wrong! . . . Where did they, how could they, get that idea? . . . Silly fools!' The critical consensus was that she was past it and a has-been.

She bore their cruel impertinence bravely. I blushed with sympathetic embarrassment and admired her outward stoicism and the humility of her stooping to lend an ear to the insults of inferiors. When the Cecils rejoined us, she remarked merely that the programme had not been interesting. Extra guests arrived for lunch, including a gentle lady don. Without warning, in the middle of the meal, Elizabeth picked upon and savaged some tentative statement made by this poor person, who was shattered.

A few years later we once more stayed together with the Cecils at Red Lion House in Cranborne. Elizabeth either had no bad feelings to relieve, or did not relieve them publicly. I believe she was happier, and remember only the warmth and the restored harmony of her relations with David and Rachel. Amongst her many gifts was the capacity for enthusiasm, vigorous and contagious, which, under pressure, I suppose, could turn into the negative force that alarmed and did damage.

Her work became increasingly obscure. Her prose grew lawless, and she was apt to throw out the baby of meaning with the bathwater of the humdrum details she had decided to dispense with: she seemed to fall foul of the occupational hazard of stylists. *The Little Girls* and *Eva Trout* bear some resemblances to the last fictional words of another fine female writer, *The Waves* by Virginia Woolf.

Time may or may not reveal the secrets of these books to future generations.

BUT TO GO back to the beginning, so to speak: the other person staying at Linton Road for the weekend of my first visit was Cynthia Asquith.

I must confess that I did not take to her immediately: she was not everyone's cup of instant tea. She and David and Rachel were 'best' friends to an almost exclusive degree; and she was more than twice my age, Lady Cynthia to me, a dignified woman, my mother's acquaintance, who had a rather abrupt manner and a disconcertingly appraising greenish eye.

She was above medium height, broad-shouldered, and carried herself well. But none of her facial characteristics ever convinced me that she had been a noted society beauty, and that she and Lady Diana Cooper were bracketed together as the Moon Goddesses. I could see no trace of beauty in her countenance, even when I got fond of it. She had had to have her teeth remodelled: they were unexpectedly large when she laughed. Her hair was hennaed, a dull red in colour, and she had it permed and done short and close to her head. Sometimes she looked a bit like a frog, sometimes like a larger aristocratic Puck, sometimes wild and sometimes tame – her variety of expressions reflected her mercurial temperament.

Her conversation was clever in quick bursts, a pithy comment here, a stimulating interpolation there – no monologues or laying down the law, and seldom an anecdote. She might have had some sympathy with feminism, but not the militant sort, although she had played the dominant role in her family life. She had been brought up in circumstances and at a time in which women wielded their power behind the scenes, and probable training had combined with natural inclination to preserve her air of mystery. She was an ex-goddess of the moon partly because of a certain remoteness.

Alas – again – I cannot remember the funny things she was always saying. She unfailingly saw the ridiculous point, she smoothed the rougher edges of reality with ridicule, and she could somehow create an exhilarating kind of jollity.

Here is a minor example of her humour which springs to mind. Perhaps at Linton Road, David or Rachel described an episode in a country house where they had recently stayed. Their host and hostess were known to Cynthia, and, by common consent, an excessively prosaic couple. But the Cecils had come down to dinner during the visit in question, and as they entered the drawing-room had been startled to overhear the unromantic husband calling his unprepossessing wife 'my little rabbit'. Cynthia listened to this story and enquired: 'Do you think he actually called her his little habit?'

On the Monday morning Cynthia and I were to travel up to London together by train from Oxford. I feared the journey would be a strain. But I heard myself chatting throughout freely and easily. My companionable companion asked questions about my writing. David and Rachel had handed back to me the typescript of *Morning*, which had been discussed during the weekend, and Cynthia now wondered if she might be allowed to borrow and read it. I hesitated: I was still in the dark in respect of her literary qualifications, if any. But then I bowed to the almost inevitable and let her have the book.

Two or three days later I received her long, professional, constructive and gratifying letter, my answer to which led to our meeting again and the start of our friendship.

That letter of hers is dated 1955. In passing, and from a sociological point of view, her mode of addressing me may be worthy of note. Notwithstanding her seniority, and our having spent three nights under the same roof, and the talk and the travel, she called me by my surname rather than my Christian name. Such formal usage has been discontinued.

Cynthia lived at 15 Queen's Gate Gardens in Kensington. Her flat was on the second floor of the large house, which had a creaking old lift in the well of the staircase. At her request I duly went there – often for tea, sometimes for supper on a telly tray, and for her dinner parties of blessed memory. At this time I myself dwelt in a couple of tiny attic rooms, reached by climbing ninety-odd stairs, and not suitable for entertaining in. Occasionally I took Cynthia out to dine in a small quiet residential hotel of her choosing: she liked to toy with the idea of getting rid of property and possessions and moving into it. She suffered from the complications of existence in general and her existence in particular, and always yearned to simplify it.

Her flat was spacious. There were three or four rooms with high ceilings, a hall, a dark little study at the back and the usual offices. The decoration was, in a word, conventional: the most unconventional people never bother to flout the conventions in ways that are, or that they consider, unimportant. I believe she had interesting pictures: am I imagining a portrait or portraits of herself? In her sitting-room were many oriental jade carvings, collected by her late husband; and books filled some waist-high bookshelves.

Our friendship was the truer for not invariably running smooth. Cynthia could be constrained and cause constraint. She could be almost too tense and jerky to communicate or to communicate with. Instead of helping to keep the conversational balloon in the air, she would sharply pop and deflate it. For reasons never given, possibly difficulties or sorrows in her emotional life, or anxiety about her two sons and her grandchildren, or money worries, or the pains of literary composition, or ill health, she would as it were retire behind the screen of her dignity and mystery.

If she had a knack of absenting herself from the social scene while present, I have a non-misanthropic tendency to shun it. I am definitely not so convivial as Charles Snow, for instance – I could not relax at a banquet. And the more I talk the less I write on the next day or days. I like talking, I prefer writing: that is the rub – I feel I understand Thomas Hardy, who, accused by his wife of not speaking to anybody in the preceding two weeks, protested that indeed he had, he had just spoken to the milkman, he had wished him good morning.

In the context of my association with Cynthia, I may not have been ever ready to sacrifice my work on the altar of an encounter that either might be bad, an exhausting conversational effort, an expense of spirit, or so good, amusing, exciting, that it used up my verbal and literary resources.

But she was prepared to do the duties of our friendship that I omitted to do. She would write the postcards and letters that I answered, she would suggest the plans and issue the invitations that I fell in with and accepted. She was infinitely polite and never demanding, and recognised and to some extent shared my dilemma, the horns of which could be labelled 'creation' and 'recreation'. The quality of hers that I found irresistible was her constancy. I had been surprised by her professional attitude to writing: I was surprised over and over again by the resourcefulness, the willingness and the steadiness of her affection.

The generation gap was bridged by common interests. At the same time Cynthia steered well clear of un-platonic quicksands.

I sat on the sofa at the foot of her bed and watched television without a moment's unease. She liked the idea of the telly tray: she preferred whimsical food, small quantities of delicacies prettily served, the type of repast to set before a doll, although she also cooked or provided solid fare for male appetites, and I never left Queen's Gate Gardens feeling hungry. After supper we would munch chocolate coffee-beans or thin chocolate biscuits shaped like leaves and tasting of almonds.

One summer evening she telephoned at about seven o'clock and asked me to hurry over, if I happened to be free, to watch the coming thunderstorm. I did so, and we moved armchairs in front of the open sitting-room window and sat there enjoying nature's meteorological spectacular.

Sometimes we met for a walk before tea: which meant promenading round and round the Gardens of Queen's Gate, the railed area of greenery and municipal flowers in front of number 15.

And exceptions merely prove the rule that our meetings

were rewarding: I have to speak for myself, and I understate the case.

If they had not rewarded me, I would not still miss her thirty years after her death.

AT CYNTHIA'S

I KNEW CYNTHIA FOR five years only. She had written and published, and she gave me, her two volumes of autobiography; but I must have read without marking, learning and inwardly digesting them. And she seldom spoke of the past, and never voiced a complaint in my hearing, except in order to make rueful fun of herself. As a result, while she was alive, I was more or less oblivious of her troubled history.

I do remember her referring to an odd link between us. My father's aunt, my late great-aunt, Lady Angela Forbes by name, had been the mistress of her father, Lord Wemyss. Apparently Lady Angela was installed as a semi-permanent member of Lord Wemyss' household, and upset Lady Wemyss especially by finding fault with the food on offer. Cynthia searched through scrapbooks for a photograph of Lady Angela, which would give me an idea of what she looked like. The one she produced had been taken at a fancy dress ball and showed a bearded figure wearing a souwester, oilskins and waders.

I also recall her reminiscences of the chow dogs her family had gone in for – their fiercely faithful natures, their expensive passion for hunting and killing other people's chickens and sheep – and her singularly sad account of the chow she had loved best, which tried to reach her by jumping over an iron railing and impaled itself on the spikes.

But I have had to learn the salient facts of her life, which surely contributed to the formation of the character and personality I knew, since she died.

She was the child of what must have been an uncomfortable union. Her mother always loved Arthur Balfour, sometime Prime Minister, who teased her platonically; her father was an unlucky gambler as well as a womaniser. The family lived beyond its means in the fine stately Wemyss house in Gloucestershire called Stanway: where, too soon, Cynthia learned the disturbing lesson that sums of money for housekeeping do not necessarily add up.

Portraits and snapshots prove the beauty of her young womanhood. She had horizontal eyebrows and gentle curving lips, an expression determinedly innocent and deceptively calm. But this Moon Goddess agreed to marry Beb Asquith, the second son of Prime Minister H. H. Asquith, and, at least in David Cecil's opinion, came down to earth with a bump.

Herbert Asquith, nicknamed Beb, does not get a good press from the friends of Cynthia who were acquainted with him and with me, as I record with apologies to his descendants. He is said to have been chilly, sarcastic, selfish, dotty, and to have had a powerful weakness for the bottle. He was a poor man into the bargain, and, understandably enough, after fighting in the 1914 war, seems to have been incapable of earning any money.

68

According to David, there was general surprise that Cynthia should wish to be his wife. But she did not change her mind in the three years of their engagement, and then she bore her husband three sons.

Whatever the war did or did not do to Beb, it killed two of Cynthia's brothers. Other sisters suffered similar, and even greater, losses. Perhaps Cynthia cannot be singled out for special sympathy. Yet I cannot help imagining the permanent damage done to her loyal and loving heart and her hyper-sensitive nervous system by those premature deaths.

A blow probably more severe was in store for her. John, her eldest son, turned out to be not right in the head. I gather, though not from Cynthia, who never mentioned him to me, that he was not to be trusted with other children or with pets. At last she took the courageous decision, after consultations with all the best doctors, to isolate him from the rest of the family and thus to protect her younger boys, Michael and Simon, from the disruption and possible danger of his company. She entrusted John to a succession of nannies and female keepers, and provided a house or flat for them by the sea in Sussex.

Her financial history was now repeating itself. Just as her youth had been burdened by the fecklessness of her father, so Beb's extravagance added to the burdens of her married life. Once she told me that Beb would go to buy an evening paper and come back with a piece of jade. Moreover, apparently, he refused to co-operate with her attempts to economise.

She buckled down to finding the necessary. She made

money by playing poker. She began to write articles for magazines. She was already an accomplished writer in a private capacity, as diarist; and she had the literary artist's gift of creating phrases that startle and haunt by means of a sort of moral perceptiveness. Here is the final sentence of her diary of the First World War years: 'One will have to look at long vistas again, instead of short ones, and one will at last fully recognise that the dead are not only dead for the duration of the war.'

But she was not the first or the last artist to discover that art does not pay: on the contrary, as a rule, artists must pay to do art.

Salvation arrived in the incongruous shape of J. M. Barrie, who contradicted the above inasmuch as he had won both international fame and an enormous fortune with his pen. Cynthia became his secretary and general factotum, and managed to help her parents as well as herself and her own family by getting him to rent her beloved Stanway and entertain them all there in the summer months.

Barrie was almost a midget, a self-made dour difficult Scottish genius, a lover of women who was incapable of fully heterosexual relationships, a lover of little boys who was not fully homosexual, a Peter Pan with a power-complex, demanding and subject to the blackest moods. He was Cynthia's 'Master', as he signed himself, for twenty-odd years, while she more than earned her wage by submitting to his sentimental dominion and seeing him through psychological crises. I believe she did not enter any detail of their association in her diary: a sign perhaps of the embarrassment it cost her to provide temporal and emotional services beyond the call of convention, contract or duty.

Mercifully her son John died – in an institution – in his twenties. Then Barrie died, and then Beb. But the financial problems they had caused and solved between them were not interred for ever in their graves. She had inherited Barrie's royalties. They made her rich in a year in which his plays were frequently performed, and poorer in years in which they were performed less often. Thus she never knew her income; her generosity inclined her to shower largesse on her offspring and dependents; and then she would receive bills for the tax on money she had spent at a time when she was receiving none.

She worried about Michael and Simon, and was no doubt saddened by the relative rift between herself and the latter. The Cecils had loved having her and Simon to stay, partly because he was such a clever and charming young man, and mother and son got on so well together. David and Rachel never knew why things had suddenly gone wrong.

A story told me with black humour by another mother may have a bearing on this one of Cynthia's various maternal vicissitudes.

The mother claimed that she and her son, who was younger than Simon at the relevant time and still at school, were real soulmates: 'I loved him dearly, he seemed to love me, I tried my hardest to make him happy and he made me happier than I've ever been, we agreed about everything and could scarcely bear to be separated. He was sixteen and coming home for the summer holidays, and I'd planned a hundred treats and was waiting

71

with bated breath to meet him at the railway station. And he stepped out of the train and said, "You've ruined my life."'

CONSIDERING CYNTHIA'S CHAPTER of existential accidents, and my experience of her intelligence and capability, the conclusion likely to be drawn from the combination of these phenomena is that she suffered from very bad luck. Obviously it was not her fault that her father was a spendthrift, her brothers were killed in the war, her husband was a casualty of the fighting, and she had a mentally deficient son. For reasons beyond our comprehension she just had to carry a heavy cross a long way. No wonder, looking back, that I found her somewhat nervy on occasions, anxious, harassed, and that despite her sex and her uniqueness could almost have included her in the mass of men who, according to Thoreau, lead lives of quiet desperation.

The tragedy of producing a child not sufficiently like others – do decent parents ever get over it?

I imagine that Cynthia's sentiments confided to her diary are representative of those of the majority of mothers in her predicament: 'Oh God, surely nothing so cruel can really have happened to me myself?'

But it had happened – it does happen. Cynthia had written that she thought her husband was mad: 'It's funny having a mad husband and a mad son.' To what extent she seriously associated Beb's abnormality – by her standards – with John's, I would not like to guess. Although more abnormal fathers have sired more normal sons than John, probability may have pointed the finger at Beb, and, anyway, it would have been superhuman of Cynthia not to do so, at least inwardly.

Nevertheless, sympathy notwithstanding, without blaming anybody and as a matter of fact, Cynthia's matrimonial and maternal tribulations are all traceable to her own agreement to marry Beb; and I would suggest that she was moved to choose him, or to agree to be chosen, not least by her innate, reckless and perhaps indescribable tendency to take the opposite line, to react, counter, and fly in the face of opinion and advice.

I am not implying that she did not love him; nor that she married him on the rebound from loving his elder brother, the so-called paragon Raymond Asquith. I would not try to squeeze her into the procrustean bed of any theory of mine deriving from our abbreviated friendship. Yet I remember hearing that everyone – everyone, as they say – believed her engagement to Beb to be a bad idea: which, judging by my observations, might well have been a good enough reason for her to marry the man.

Fairly soon after we met she read an essay I had written entitled *Tolstoy, Marriage and Anna Karenina*. Tolstoy was the strongest influence on my literary youth; and I was convinced that the cause of the miserable matrimonial drama enacted at Yasnaya Polyana was not the selfishness of his attempt to live like a poor peasant instead of a rich and famous aristocratic writer, but the chronic failure of Countess Tolstoy – his wife Sonya – to understand the nature of his genius and his religious aspirations, or to adapt to his spiritual development. Certain episodes in *Anna Karenina* seemed to support my argument.

Cynthia wrote on a postcard from Stockholm that she was 'enthralled' by the essay; also, incidentally, that she was 'surrounded by the most placid-looking population ever seen'. She then reacted against my interpretation of the Tolstoys' marriage: she begged to differ, she teased me by differing – it was a fey, wise, corrective, diplomatic joke, more than contradiction. But I was persuaded, as were the Cecils, that her disagreement with me was part of the inspiration of her book on the subject, *Married to Tolstoy*.

She was working on her apology for, and defence of, Sonya Tolstoy throughout the years we were friends. Our shared preoccupation with the Tolstoys was an additional bond, cemented by her humour. We lent each other biographical books by Leo Tolstoy's first English translator Aylmer Maude, by Tolstoy's sister-in-law Tanya, who is supposed to have been the model for Natasha in *War and Peace*, by four of Tolstoy's children, and so on.

Cynthia addressed me thus in a letter from Brighton: 'My dear Aylmer, or may I call you Maude?' She continues: 'You don't really mean to tell me my clean copy of Simmons' *Leo Tolstoy* is yours? Well I never! I have carefully read, completely forgotten the contents of, and recently rubbed out all I had written in another copy, and, I thought, returned it to you. But it must have belonged and gone home to the London Library. Anyhow, this one has not yet written my name in itself even in pencil, and you shall have it – but NOT YET!' She manages to introduce comedy into this question of the ownership of books: 'By the way, your letter gave me a nasty shock by inquiring for the safety of Leon's *Tolstoy, His Life and Work*. Have I your copy? I thought it was my own, acquired second-hand. It has my name in it, but admittedly in my handwriting (only pencilled). I suppose it is yours. At all events it is safe, if not sound.' Back in Brighton she finds herself in bleak weather – she refers to the difficulty of distinguishing sea from sky – and 'a FOG of DESPAIR . . . I get more and more exhaustingly lost in the impenetrable jungle of material in all these books, each of which flatly contradicts the last, even about matters so objective as dates. Sonya's own son Leo and her daughter Alexandra cannot agree about the year of her death.' This Brighton letter is typewritten and includes the sentence: 'Forgive rather stronly individyal typewriting.'

At a later stage of the work on *Married to Tolstoy* Cynthia began to sign herself Sonya, and to call me Chertkov, the friend of Tolstoy and fanatical leader of the Tolstoyan faction opposed to his wife, and variously described as Tolstoy's chief apostle, guardian angel, evil genius, black shadow, and saint, hypocrite and devil.

Her fun epistolary and otherwise had a serious side, and the ingredient of gallantry in her high spirits was edifying. Moreover a mere inclination to refute does not usually inspire scrupulous historical research and a book judged by cognoscenti to be among the best of many on the same subject. Whether the naive blame I unjustly heaped on Countess Tolstoy's head provoked Cynthia to set the record straighter is not only a moot point, but perhaps beside the point: which is that she had written about a dozen books of considerable interest before the Tolstoy one, and the hundreds of thousands of words of her classic diary.

To have been wife and mother and provider for her family; to have banished John for the sake of others, and braved doubt and the facile criticism of outsiders; to have stood by her husband through thick rather than thin, and by Barrie too; to have been the comfort and joy of her parents and countless friends; to have borne the loss and fear of the loss of loved ones in two wars; and still to have written so much and so well – to have done all this argues a character more steadfast and stoical than hers appeared to be at first glance.

No – she was born an aristocrat, and to be idle and rich, and became a classless professional, working overtime to keep wolves from doors and realise her potential even as she approached the age of seventy. Although life had not exactly been kind to her, she forgave it, she revelled in it, and broadcast the glad tidings of her enjoyment. Her talent for frivolity had deep roots.

I hope she would not take exception to a compliment meant to be the reverse of backhanded: the biggest surprise she ever sprung on me was permitting me to discover that she was a brick.

Married to Tolstoy, the finished article, betrays her complexity – or David and Rachel and I thought it did. The book surely benefits from not ending quite as it begins: it is more balanced and even-handed. The author, we suspected, fell out of sympathy with the wronged wife

Sonya and in love with the oppressive husband, Tolstoy himself.

CYNTHIA ATTENDED DAVID and Rachel's wedding, at which, she wrote, they looked 'like royal children'.

She had been another of the 'best' female friends of David as bachelor: who probably introduced her to one of his 'best' male friends, Leslie Hartley. Cynthia and Leslie then became 'best' friends, and Rachel, despite her later arrival on the scene, somehow succeeded in squaring the triangle of 'best' friendship.

Cynthia and Rachel's relationship might have got off to a bad start if tolerance and common sense had been in shorter supply, for Rachel's father Desmond MacCarthy had loved Cynthia for years, and her mother had been caused much heartache in consequence.

But I was always hazy about Rachel's attitude to her parents, and most of her pre-marital existence for that matter. The vague impression I received was that she admired her father, was charmed by and fond of him, sometimes in spite of herself, and that she had the usual difficulties of daughters in her relations with her mother. If so, if she was more on her father's side, she might not have objected strongly to the part Cynthia played in her girlhood.

Anyway, when I got to know Rachel, she was as close as David was to Cynthia. One of the latter's memorable phrases, appreciative and descriptive of David's wife, was that she was lovely to talk to because she not only retrieved and returned the conversational ball, but skimmed it back with a nicely-judged little cut.

Rachel was greatly intrigued by the privacy of Cynthia's love-life, no doubt partly owing to Desmond MacCarthy's attachment to her, and the question of whether or not it had been platonic. Her curiosity was also sharpened when, staying somewhere with Cynthia, she discovered in a book a letter penned with passion to Cynthia by a man who had seemed to be no more than her slight acquaintance. How much the Cecils knew about her relations with Collin Brooks, and how much there was to know, I cannot say. I came across his name for the first time, and saw it coupled with Cynthia's, only recently, although they must have cared for each other for three of the five years in which I considered myself her confidant. Collin Brooks was ill and died at the end of that three-year period, and again I was unaware of her grief.

Of Leslie Hartley, on the other hand, Cynthia talked to me often before I met him – and afterwards. Perhaps it was natural that she should do so without reserve since she was not tongue-tied by romantic interest in him. Perhaps it was also ironical, for I believe no one could have loved her more than he did in his fashion.

Needless to say Cynthia referred to his looks. She took people at face value to an amazing extent. She was snobbish about nothing except the physical appearance of human beings: these criteria of hers seemed to have no connection with her having been beautiful once upon a time, or with having ceased to be beautiful in early middle age – if she was vain, her vanity never obtruded. To begin with, when she discussed somebody's jawline, or nostrils or earlobes or length of upper lip, I thought erroneously that she was joking.

In the case of Leslie's countenance, she as it were picked out his eyes. She compared his general appearance to that of a seal: and rightly, for his outline had a sleek seal-like rotundity, and his smooth dogged face and bald head were reminiscent of a seal surfacing in the sea. The comparison was reinforced by the fact that he liked to swim and to row: water was really his element, she told me. From a less zoological point of view, he had a look of H. G. Wells. But his eyes were indeed incomparable – very blue, dreamy and perspicacious, and so vital and vivid as to merit the metaphorical epithet 'hot'. While he might have been able to lose himself in a crowd, to pose as the average man and escape attention, his eyes 'gave away his genius', according to Cynthia's graphic description.

Leslie lived beside water. The river Avon flowed through the garden of his home, which was near Bath, and only a few miles from Claverton, where Cynthia had lived until Beb died and she moved to Queen's Gate Gardens. I went there once later on. As I remember, the house reared up from the inside edge of the pavement bordering a busy main road; but passing through a door in the high garden wall was like gaining admission to another, better world. Peace reigned, relatively speaking; the Bath stone of the generous Victorian edifice seemed cleaner and more golden; and the grounds were extensive and orderly. The sitting-room was on the first floor, reached via a stair-well hung with the silken rugs that Leslie collected – more rugs were draped over the banisters. It was cosy and airy, had fine china in glass showcases ranged around, and possibly a large bow-window, and certainly a spectacular view. Mown lawn sloped down to the tree-fringed bank of the darkly glassy river. The meadows beyond it were slashed diagonally with the old green earthworks of a railway viaduct, along which, in Leslie's days, steam trains puffed and hooted with romantic implications. And in the farther distance the villa-strewn hills enclosed the landscape. Altogether it reminded me of those gaudy thirties-style posters advertising rail travel through idealised scenery.

Leslie paid visits to London, and invited Cynthia to stay in the country. He was a hard worker – apart from his many novels, he must have produced thousands of book reviews; and she was as interested as every other writer is in a colleague's method of composition. She thought that Leslie's competed with Joyce Cary's for the prize of strangeness, and was much more enviable. She said that he sat at a table or desk in the window of his sitting-room, writing with a fountain-pen when she and even when any number of other guests were present: he needed neither solitude nor silence in which to perform his act of creation. Moreover he would write half a page without stopping or crossing out a single word, then merely raise his head and touch his chin with the blunt end of his pen before settling down to cover the other half of the page with his elegant handwriting.

He not only never blotted a line. On one occasion I ventured to ask him a technical question: how much, and in what way, did he revise his books? He replied rather apologetically that he hardly revised them at all: his manuscripts were typed and sent to the publisher, and he confined expensive alterations to the proofs to a minimum.

Leslie had every reason to be bored by my interrogation and might have been teasing me. Equally he might have been telling the truth, for he was blessed with the inability to be dull on paper, and his story-telling is noted for its spontaneity.

To Cynthia I put another question some time after meeting Leslie: would he like to read my book, should I present him with a copy of *Morning* by way of tribute? She advised me not to.

'He reads nothing nowadays if he can help it, except the Bible.'

CYNTHIA WAS SOCIABLE as well as reclusive, and hospitable despite straitened means, and gave dinner parties, in several of which she included me.

As a rule the company consisted of the foursome of 'best' friends, the hostess, Leslie and the Cecils, and myself and another guest of the opposite sex, making even numbers of men and women.

I remember three of these extra ladies. One was nice-looking and well-behaved, attentive to the talk, contributing her acceptable mite to it, seeing the jokes and so on.

But then Cynthia got hold of some intense Greek poetess, rumpled, haggard and humourless, who greeted David Cecil thus in broken English: 'Your brother has the title – no?' She interrupted the conversation and brayed with laughter at anything that was not intended to amuse.

Alone with Cynthia at a later meeting I complained of the poetess, and received the immediately reactive and roguish reply: 'How odd! She was meant to be a treat for you. I'm told no Greek man can resist her.'

However, Cynthia relented to the extent of inviting another lady of her acquaintance to the next dinner party. This one was a wispy beaded Civil Servant with literary leanings, who took the shine off the stars of the evening by insistently trying to discuss other modern authors with them.

Again, encouraged by David and Rachel, I protested to Cynthia. But she brushed aside our objections and carried her characteristic joke a stage further with a startling recommendation of the lady in question: 'I can assure you that she's considered a sibyl in our Kensingtonian circle.'

A faithful female retainer came in to cook the dinner for her parties, and to wait at table. She would also open the front door of the flat and usher guests into the sitting-room.

I retain a picture in my mind's eye of Cynthia welcoming us with open arms, tall and erect, her smile combining dignity and impudence, dignity and puckishness at any rate, standing centrally so that she could check on her appearance in the mirror over the mantelpiece, and conferring on each of us the freedom of her drinks tray.

Rachel sits on the sofa on one side of the electric fire in the grate, neat as a new pin, looking absurdly girlish in her middle-age and deceptively prim, and wearing a contradictorily adult and sophisticated piece of priceless Cecil jewellery. David seems to be trying to drink, smoke and talk all at the same time. He has taken up his favourite position in front of the fire, and is demonstrating another of his accomplishments, the rare one in a sober writer of being able to get a party going. With the assistance of Cynthia's prompting queries, he burbles along, laughing, telling, asking, drawing everybody in and out, and setting an un-English example in not sticking in the mud of shyness and reserve. Even the extra guest cannot spoil the sport he mainly helps to set in train.

Leslie was apt to arrive late. I see him in a smooth grey double-breasted suit, shaking hands with a lovable grin but without small talk, hurrying to fetch a drink and extract a cigarette from his rectangular gold cigarette case – unlike David, whose cigarettes emerged more or less scathed from crumpled packets. He has noticeably long brown fingers with nicely-shaped nails, a countrified out-door complexion, and a look of health and fitness which he probably owes to his rowing.

We would cross the windowless hall of the flat to the traditional dining-room with mahogany table, chairs and sideboard.

Leslie's form of humour differed from Cynthia's plays on words, and waggish interjections, and intellectually knockabout style; and from Rachel's gentle mockery of life in general; and even from David's wide range of comic conversational effects. It was as understated as it was original. I have heard people say he was not good company: my interpretation of which statement is that such people did not permit him to make his humorous point, or were too dense to see it. When he began to speak quietly in his tentative diffident voice, Cynthia and the Cecils were pleased to stop talking and to listen. His recent experience, usually mortifying, was the raw material of his drollery. For example, I remember him saying he had attended some international literary gathering, where the Romanian delegate approached him and asked his opinion of the work of Gramgren. He had never heard of this writer, but did not wish to betray his ignorance of – probably – the European avant-garde and its new champion, and therefore hesitated. The Romanian repeated the name reproachfully and with increasing vehemence – 'Gramgren! Gramgren!' – until Leslie finally realised he was referring to Graham Greene.

But his rendering of a heavy Romanian accent, and the subtlety of his narration of the episode and his physical expressiveness, defeat my descriptive powers. Verbally, as in his books, he was a past master at presenting himself as the victim of laughable embarrassment, misunderstanding, doubt and fear.

The saga of the swans' nest in Leslie's garden kept his friends amused for weeks. The swans had chosen to nest by the mooring for his boat, and fiercely prevented him getting into it and going for a row. He was unable to scare them off – on the contrary, they did the scaring. At length he tried to poison them, although they belonged to the monarch, and he suspected that penalties of medieval savagery might be visited on anyone doing a swan injury.

But the poison acted like a tonic. With the greatest difficulty he then obtained china eggs of the correct magnitude and substituted them for the genuine article, so that at least the swans would never have cygnets to defend; but they sat upon and guarded these eggs five times longer than would have been the case with the real ones.

Another saga was his clash with his publisher, who expressed reservations about one of his books: I think it was his telling satire on socialism called *Facial Justice*, the theme of which is that in a brave new egalitarian world everyone would have to be made to look alike by means of plastic surgery.

Leslie's version of events was that his publisher had invited him to dinner with a lot of other people and in the middle of the meal had shouted across the table that neither he nor any of his readers liked the book. Leslie's consequent assumption was that it had been rejected, and he must try to find someone else to publish it and his future work. But his publisher, having heard of opportunistic rivals queueing up to offer Leslie ever larger sums of money to sign on their dotted lines, returned to the charge: he retracted, grovelled, and was forced to pay an unprecedented advance to retain an author who might have been his for comparatively next to nothing.

This story was a trifle untypical in that Leslie figured in it as a David versus a Goliath, instead of just a smaller milder man trampled on by bigger persons and by circumstances out of control.

One setting of the Dutch auction for his literary output was the dining-room at Queen's Gate Gardens. The

Cecils were unable to attend this particular dinner party, and Cynthia had invited an old friend in publishing to help to fill their places – Daniel George, maybe. After the ladies had left the room, Leslie was subjected to a barrage of tempting propositions by our fellow-guest.

As it happened, I had by this time written A *Letter*, and was in the process of losing my illusions in respect of publishers. Perhaps they were not the disinterested lovers of literature in general and my books in particular I had thought they were, and the reward they looked for was not just to be of service to humanity and poor authors. I was wondering how many more months I could wait to know whether a fraction of the profit made on my first book would be invested in my second.

At some stage I therefore piped up to say that I too might be in need of a new publisher, and was swatted down by the response of the representative of the publishing industry sitting opposite me: 'You're a beginner.'

The snub might have been deserved; but that is not the point of my reminiscence. I record it here because Leslie and David never did and never would have administered it there. When we three sat together at Cynthia's dining-table, I was not judged by my years or lack of them, by how much work I had published or by how much money I had been paid for it, I was neither condescended to nor patronised, but treated as if I were the others' equal, and not even made to feel I was intruding upon their old-established friendship.

Rachel and Cynthia and I had become friends without delay or difficulty; but difference of sex also bridges generation gaps, and the competitive element is less inclined to elbow its way into the relations of men with women. David and Leslie proved yet again how exceptional they were by being so nice to me when I was 'beginning'.

At Cynthia's dinner parties, which I enjoyed more than any before or since, we three would rejoin the ladies in the sitting-room. The social atmosphere was a mixture of good sense and goodwill, of first-rate bonhomous rationality. The jokes seemed to get better and better, and the flash of every form of wit more dazzling. Reluctantly I took my leave, and was pleased to dally on the stairs or in the unsteady lift while Cynthia kept things going for as long as she could with wild and catching jollity. In the street below, walking home, I decided that she and Leslie and Rachel and David were the finest and funniest people in the whole wide world.

Cynthia cannot have found it easy to unwind and to sleep after her parties and all she put into them. No doubt she had recourse to her bottle of sleeping pills: it was actually more a jar than a bottle, the sort of kitchen jar in which a pound of rice is usually stored. She had shown it to me, rattling the two or three hundred pills of many colours and shapes inside.

'Aren't they pretty?' she asked me. 'And they have such deep emotional appeal.'

PSYCHIATRY WOULD, AND does, persuade people to say everything that is on their minds and to get everything off their chests. By tacit agreement, Cynthia and I begged to differ from such dangerous claptrap. Setting aside considerations of good behaviour and good manners, we guarded each other's privacy: which is perhaps the first and last duty of friendship.

But my second novel was written in the form of an epistle to a woman loved, whence its title *A Letter*. It begins: 'We were by the sea, do you remember?' I discussed the book with Cynthia while my publisher dawdled.

Thereafter she was apt to greet me with a pair of questions: 'How are you? And how is "you"?'

Her joke was self-sufficient, surely not intended to invite or provoke revelations. And she never revealed to me her depression when she at last completed *Married to Tolstoy*. The work had been a marathon, exhausting, and a lot of it was done when she was distressed by Collin Brooks' fatal illness.

Putting two and two together now, and being wise after the event, Collin Brooks' death may have had something to do with a visit to a wigmaker in the company of her erstwhile daughter-in-law, her son Michael's ex-wife Didy. Cynthia wanted to try on grey wigs in order to see what she would look like if she allowed her hair to go grey.

At about this time she asked me to help her to entertain a dim old couple she had to have to dinner. I found that party rather embarrassing. The hostess was in febrile high spirits, and at her most reactive and puckish; and although her other guests did not deserve such sympathy, for he was pompous as well as dim and his spouse was a crass snob, she reminded me uneasily of a clever dog running rings round cattle and snapping at their heels.

Finished copies of *A Letter* came through and I gave her one, and then heard she was not well.

A day or two later she was dead.

She had been staying with Didy and her grandchildren in the country: actually in Gloucestershire, very near Stanway. She had arrived with a headachey cold, which got worse and turned into meningitis; and she died in hospital in Oxford.

I received her posthumous message via Didy that she was looking forward to reading my book.

There was a Memorial Service at St Martin's-in-the-Fields, and Leslie agreed to deliver the funerary oration. How he managed to do it, and so beautifully and bravely, I cannot imagine. He was paler than I had ever seen him, but his voice did not shake too much as he said his last goodbye from the pulpit.

Here is part of what he read out to the large congregation: 'One cannot think of her apart from her physical presence and the beauty, sunshiny at one moment, moonlit the next, that was as various and unpredictable as her talk. But I won't say more of the physical and mental graces that were the vesture of her spirit, and that are, for each of her friends, a treasured possession, not to be disturbed by any attempt of mine to paint the lily. You could truly say of her, in the words of Shakespeare, whose plays she knew almost by heart, that a star danced when she was born and went on dancing till she died.

'But underlying these gossamer qualities that so delighted the eye and ear . . . was a stable bedrock of character and a strong practical sense that made her, among many other things, the most reliable and dependable of friends. To them she gave herself, and her time, unstintingly. No journey was too long for her to take, if at the end of it she could help someone; no engagement too trifling or inconvenient to keep; no responsibility too heavy to shoulder. And this conscientiousness in private and public matters . . . she carried into her work as a writer. Modest about her own literary gifts, though always ready to encourage other people's, she was a most scrupulous craftsman, and never more so than in her last book, which she has not lived to see published: the life of Countess Tolstoy. She revised it and revised it, and it may be her finest and most lasting memorial, for into it she put the faith and hope that burned in her, and the charity that informed all her judgments.'

Leslie's closing paragraph includes the following sentences: 'It was her special gift to be ironically detached from herself and yet vitally concerned with other people. She saw herself in a mirror, often as a figure of fun. Perhaps we saw her in a mirror too, for in spite of her directness she had a mysteriousness, a quality that was not quite of this world.'

APOLOGY FOR CYNTHIA

I REMEMBER HAVING LUNCH with Leslie before Cynthia died. He asked me to come to a flat in a building in Knightsbridge: I think he was renting the flat temporarily, but it was so comfortable that he might have furnished it himself and lived there for ages when in London.

The day was sunny and pretty. I arrived and took a lift to a higher floor and found that my fellow-guests were Cynthia and C. V. Wedgwood the historian, Veronica Wedgwood, later created a Dame of the British Empire and a member of the Order of Merit. Soon the four of us were seated at a white-clothed table near a window, through which the sun shone, but without dazzling. Delicious food was served, and Leslie dispensed wine from an antique glass decanter shaped like a seal resting on its flippers.

He had the good host's talent for looking calm and contented. He exuded well-being and eupepsia. Over coffee, he and I piled Pelion upon the Ossa of pleasure by lighting our cigarettes; and I have an idea that Leslie, later, produced and unrolled a leather-covered tobacco-pouch, ruminatively filled an elegant long-stemmed pipe, lit it and puffed out sweetly aromatic smoke. He was an inveterate smoker: he told me he would smoke anything, leaves, rope, if he could not get tobacco.

The afternoon advanced. The sunlight fell on what was now the still life of the luncheon table: the bowl of fruit, the partly eaten bunch of grapes with bloom intact, the fruit-plates and coffee-cups and moist silver cream jug and glasses showing a residue of wine. And we continued to talk, though by no means exclusively shop, even if the craft and profession we had in common promoted an easy and warm sense of comradeship. Perhaps I do not speak only for myself in saying I was loth to break the golden thread of sociability linking us together; to close my ears to the harmony of the civilised chorus of those kindred spirits; to spurn the good luck of being there, and, in short, get up and go.

I was younger than the others – no doubt hero-worship heightened my enjoyment of the occasion; and then Cynthia and Leslie, remarkably considering how busy they were and their years of age, seemed so carefree and regardless of time.

How long before time exacted its revenge?

I forget – and as Rachel put it in a letter to me, 'One cannot connect Cynthia with death at all.'

Rachel wrote from Linton Road: 'So strange that she should have died in Oxford, and that we never even knew she was ill . . . We went to her funeral . . . The church was huge and gloomy . . . Michael and Simon stood like statues in the front, and there was something endearing about their tragic hopelessness . . . Lady L. provided a little comic relief by arriving rather late and very *affairée* with a great sheaf of madonna lilies which she held like a baby.'

Of Simon Asquith, Rachel wrote in another letter: 'He still has a sort of battered nobility about the head – at least I thought so at the funeral.'

Married to Tolstoy came out in due course. One more tragedy of the artistic life was that the author did not live to reap the reward of her protracted work on it and her exhaustive revision. Rachel, who ended by knowing the works of Tolstoy and his matrimonial and domestic history inside out, wrote about the book: 'It is so good – much the fairest account of Countess Tolstoy – extremely well put together and so humorous. [Humour is] the only way to take their [the Tolstoys'] extraordinary way over diaries. Even daughter Tanya used to give her diary to her father to read, and then write in it that her father thought less well of her afterwards.' Leslie made a similar point: 'In telling the tragic story of two people [Tolstoy and his wife] who, in their relations with each other, had almost no sense of justice or of humour, [Cynthia] kept hers intact, and with no lessening of sympathy for either of the unhappy protagonists.'

Leslie survived Cynthia by twelve years. He must have missed her terribly; and with respect and regret I fear he may have died in – or of – a prolonged bout of depression. We met only two or three times in this last period of his life – certainly not by choice on my side, nor on his, I believe and hope, but because the usual extraneous factors got in the way. He put on more weight and talked less than he had done. His friends remarked upon the length of his pauses during telephonic conversations.

One of our chance meetings was again at a dinner party: but how different it was from Cynthia's at Queen's Gate Gardens! The host and the hostess and four or five other guests hailed from Grub Street, and the subject under discussion was exclusively the judging of the Nobel Prize for Literature, and the possibility of Leslie winning it. Although he grinned and gazed around benevolently, he seemed bemused by the hard loud professional gossip, and I was still innocent enough to be shocked to hear of the non-literary reasons for which such prizes are almost always awarded.

He did not win the Nobel Prize. He was such a modest man that he himself probably under-estimated the highest achievements of his career: the originality and quiet fascination of his rambling 'autobiographical' novel *The Boat*; the unparalleled excellence of the scenes between Eustace and Hilda when they are children in his trilogy bearing their names; and the oblique, child's-eye view of romance and drama in *The Go-between*. But, depressed or not, he continued to write books. He was prolific, he retained his facility, sitting no doubt at the table in the window of his home, raising his heavier seal-like head to look out at the restless river and the railway line and the hills and sky, touching his chin with the end of his fountain-pen and re-applying his mind and hand to the task without further hesitation.

He and David spoke to each other for hours on the telephone. The Cecils worried about, and did all they could to alleviate, his lonely old bachelorhood and isolation. David's theory was that now, if not previously, his writing was the means of telling himself a story, which

94

released him from the chafing bonds of reality and transported him into a fictional world, freer and yet more controllable than the real one.

He had appointed his 'best' friend as one of the executors of his will. After his death, the Cecils therefore had to go on business to Leslie's house in Bath. Rachel wrote to me that she was 'moved to see it again, looking quite untouched, exactly as if he was living there, the heating on, and the furniture polished and arranged just as he always had it – the Persian silk rugs on the walls, and the china given him by an aunt.'

She continued, referring to the troubles and the illness of Leslie's last years: 'Somehow all of it slips away, and one remembers only the many many visits and walks and talks and delightful times.'

DAVID BOUGHT RED Lion House in Cranborne village at a knock-down price from his brother Bobbety, Lord Salisbury. Then he and Rachel, probably to be able to afford a second home, sold 7 Linton Road and moved into a smaller house in Charlbury Road in Oxford.

They began to spend at least the university vacations in Cranborne; they invited me there for weekends; and, on the Friday afternoon of one such visit, greeted me with the news of an exciting literary discovery. Apparently Cynthia had kept a diary for most of her life. Some of it had been typed and sent to them. And it was marvellous, they said.

I remember six or eight volumes of typescript bound in dark-coloured paper piled up on the central table in the hall at Red Lion House, waiting for me. I read four or five of them in the next two days, and quite agreed with the Cecils. We all wished we had been able to tell Cynthia that she had written a masterpiece. We felt we should have known that she was cut out to be a diarist, for she loved both society and solitude, had the requisite literary qualifications, and the sound judgment, the judicial vision – but detached rather than disapproving – which enabled her to reveal people and events in an arresting perspective. And then again, useful in this as in every other context, she had her humorous lightness of touch.

We also realised that the diary would need careful editing. What Michael or Simon had sent the Cecils seemed to be a small part of a very large whole; and some experienced person would have to sift the relative dross from the gold, and plan the publication volume by volume over the next few years. I understood David to say that he would be prepared either to undertake, or supervise, the work.

Several months passed, and it transpired that Michael and Simon had decided to do the editing themselves. The portion they chose to publish covered the years of the First World War. I read the book with disappointment, and was sadly certain that the rest of the diary would never see the light of day.

The portrait of Cynthia projected by the printed page

was of some cold-hearted social butterfly, fluttering from flower to flower to scrounge honey, pleasure and fun, while her husband fought for king and country and her brothers and male relations and friends perished in the trenches. For once I could hardly disagree with the critics when they found fault with the character of the diarist.

And I was right: no more of the diary was published or will be, though not just because, as I had guessed, Michael and Simon's version discouraged a repeat performance. The unpublished remainder suffered a fate with a touch of Cynthia's own mystery. Together with other papers of hers, it was burned in a warehouse where Michael had stored it. Yet letters apparently burned in the same warehouse fire were later sold by a bookseller in Bournemouth.

Was I, were David and Rachel and one or two other literary folk to my knowledge, completely wrong about the merit of the partial typescript of the diary? Had we not read enough of the part that was edited and published to judge it? Would we have revised our opinion if we had been able to compare Cynthia's original with her sons' edition, and decided after all that there was not much difference between them?

Two more alternative questions, or perhaps answers in question form, are: did Michael and Simon lack the editorial experience that would even have improved the diary? Or were they, by means of it, trying to portray their mother as they saw her?

I can imagine that Cynthia was better as friend than as mother. Young persons generally do not appreciate the qualities that certain adults loved her for, subtlety and sophistication, for instance, and her tendency to tease and disconcert. Children are like animals, staunch conservatives: they rarely want even bad things to change, they want to know who they are, where they stand, what to expect. But Cynthia, on the surface, was changeability personified. And considering her chronic sense of harassment and shortage of time and energy when I knew her and she had few external responsibilities, she must have been less able to create an atmosphere of settled calm and contentment when she had a difficult husband, a very sick son, and the odd half-dozen hungry mouths to feed.

David and Rachel, notwithstanding their admiration of Cynthia, entertained considerable sympathy for her children for extra reasons. They said she wanted to show them off – wanted them to show off: they brought out a streak of vanity in her, and the competitive instinct, which was usually restrained by her generosity. She insisted on recitations and performances: above all, on their looking beautiful. In her muddling way, she not only asked them to compete partly on her account and win prizes, she also competed against them. The Cecils described the embarrassing spectacle of Cynthia battling like a tigress to beat little Michael and Simon and some of their juvenile contemporaries at Racing Demon.

Her competitive instinct reasserted itself when she went in for and won a series of TV Quizzes and £3200, answering questions on her chosen subject of Jane Austen's novels.

Another probably disturbing influence which she introduced into the young lives of Michael and Simon was J. M. Barrie. There is no question that she was in need of the salary he paid her: she did not enter his employment to pass the time or amuse herself. Moreover he was sympathetic and provided her family with all sorts of fringe benefits. But his relationship with her, seen from the outside, across the gulf of years, inferentially and potentially, was a can of psychological worms. It was a weird and almost complete reconstruction and repetition of that which he had had with Sylvia Llewelyn Davies and her boys, who formed the composite model of the children spirited away to Never-Neverland by Peter Pan.

Barrie in a manner of speaking stole into the Llewelyn Davies household and out of it with those boys, one of whom, Peter by name, was later to write a book about it all entitled *The Morgue*. Barrie's marriage failed, he was divorced on the grounds of non-consummation, he reserved his passion for other men's wives – specifically, mothers with husbands and very young children; and when Mr Llewelyn Davies and then Sylvia died, he made himself indispensable to the Asquiths with his fame and great wealth, and his insidiously dominating personality.

That Cynthia scented danger may be indicated by the fact that she never let Barrie meet her son John. And I – for one – can see her struggling to protect Michael and Simon from what seems to have been the emotionally seductive and destructive effect of Barrie's interest and patronage.

Still more questions cross my mind: did she not altogether succeed? Was she blamed for exposing and for having exposed her family to the force of Barrie's complexity? Were her sacrifices of herself to Barrie for

99

the sake of her family mistaken for acts of infidelity and neglect?

Was she, in short, a prophet without honour in her own country? Had she trodden on the toes of her nearest and dearest, whose representatives, Michael and Simon, used her own words to inculpate her?

The only unarguable fact is that the diary as published was not so marvellous as the Cecils, amongst others, believed it would and should have been. Cynthia's biographer Nicola Beauman sums up what was wrong with it: 'The editors made her appear harder and flightier than she really was.'

CYNTHIA ALSO SEEMS to me to have had bad posthumous luck in another context. Some years after her death, verbal aspersions cast upon her treatment of John reached my ears. The burden of the gossip was that she never should have separated John from his parents and brothers: he was not as mad as all that, and he might have benefited greatly and lived longer if he had not been excluded almost in babyhood from the family circle.

Such opinions were aired mainly by sentimental liberals of generations younger than Cynthia's – upper and middle-class post-nanny generations – who were forced to make a virtue of the necessity of looking after their children. The mothers in question were apt to become fanatical proselytisers of practical maternity, and to be down on anyone who had wriggled or did wriggle out of its chores.

I understand that nowadays quite a lot of women can again afford nannies – career women in particular need them and have no doctrinaire objection to employing them; and that other women, recognising the advantages of the job and not suffering from inverted snobbery, have seen fit to supply the demand. But in the heyday of crippling taxation and egalitarian pipe-dreams, nannies became an endangered species; and their frustrated would-be mistresses posed as earth-mothers and boasted about the psychological joy and sociological duty of 'bonding' with their offspring in all circumstances.

Their criticism of Cynthia as the mother of John is resurrected by Nicola Beauman, who widens its scope.

My guess is that Cynthia, on the whole, would have been thrilled to be the subject of Mrs Beauman's long, well-informed and interesting biography.

And despite the writer's dark hint that my uncle Charles Lister, the distinguished New Elizabethan killed in the Gallipoli campaign, was illegitimate and Cynthia's half-brother, I feel grateful to her for telling me so many things I did not know, indisputable facts about Cynthia's life and loves, and for her quotations from private papers.

Thus, for a single small instance, I gather that Cynthia had already written a play about Sonya Tolstoy before I gave her my anti-Sonya essay to react against: I probably exerted less influence than I have imagined on the writing of *Married to Tolstoy*.

But Mrs Beauman is dismissive of *Married to Tolstoy*. Although Leslie Hartley considered that it might be

Cynthia's finest and most lasting memorial, she gives it short shrift in a few hundred words in a book of roughly a hundred and thirty thousand.

She also declares that the impoverished mother of John, the same Cynthia who bravely earned the wherewithal to keep the family solvent, was 'incapable of putting herself aside . . . [and] ignoring the worldly and materialistic in order to concentrate on her child.' On the other hand she bemoans the fact that if only John's mother had followed the advice of D. H. Lawrence 'she would have tried not to *care* so much.' She disapproves more or less of all the choices appertaining to John made by Cynthia: where he lived, who looked after him, the innumerable doctors he was examined by, the school he was sent to, the institution in which he ended his short life. She opines that there was not much wrong with John, apart from Cynthia wanting him to be 'normal' and 'able to go out to tea without stuffing the entire scone in his mouth'; and wisely after the event prescribes that 'John should have had the constant, calm, loving attention of one person. He should have stayed in one place and that place should have been the country . . .'

'It is unbearable,' Mrs Beauman concludes with confidence, 'that thousands and thousands of Johns have been bundled away in institutions, sedated and half-alive, left to a fate which compassion and psychiatry and more enlightened mothering might have warded off.'

She quotes D. H. Lawrence at some length in support of her argument. Lawrence and his wife and Cynthia became friends; but, in spite of Cynthia telling me more than once that Lawrence was charming and had always been very nice to her, I think his letter of advice about John is bossy and destructive. '*Don't* try to make him love you, or obey you – don't do it . . . That you fight [for John's love] is only a sign that you are wanting in yourself,' he wrote. 'The child knows that. Your own soul is deficient, so it fights for the love of the child. And the child's soul . . . laughs at you and defies you, almost jeers at you, almost hates you.'

His next sentence: 'The great thing is, *not* to exert authority unnecessarily over the child – no prerogative, only the prerogative of pure justice' – is again unhelpful in that it restricts parental authority, it virtually denies parents any educative control of their children, since 'pure justice' is a contradiction in terms and an unattainable ideal.

Mrs Beauman has recourse to the writings of D. H. Lawrence to make a rather different point. There is a quote from Lawrence's *The Ladybird* on the back of the dust jacket, including these descriptive phrases: 'She had been one of the beauties . . . Sorrow, pain, thwarted passion had done her great damage . . . Alas! her beauty was a failure . . . Her eyes were the saddest part of her.' And one of the four epigraphs inside the book, on a page entitled *Frontpiece*, is a quotation from Lawrence's *The Rocking-Horse Winner*. Here is part of it: 'She had bonny children, yet felt they had been thrust upon her, and she could not love them . . . When her children were present, she always felt the centre of her heart go hard. This troubled her, and in her manner she was all the more gentle and anxious for her children, as if she loved them very much. Only she herself knew that at the centre of her heart was a hard little place that could not feel love, no, not for anybody.'

These two descriptions are presented, the first under a portrait of Cynthia, the second at the beginning of a biography of Cynthia, as if they really did describe Cynthia herself. But they are both fiction. Lawrence may or may not have had Cynthia in mind when he wrote the passages: who knows? The fact remains that he was creating a couple of pretty awful women, damaged, heart- less and hypocritical, to fit in with, and advance the action of, the respective yarns he wished to spin.

JOHN ASQUITH'S FATHER is not included in the charge of doing him wrong which is levelled against his mother: at least I have never seen or heard Beb's name canvassed in this context.

Yet Beb seems to me a valuable witness for the defence, as it were, in the case against Cynthia.

Historical speculation about the character of Beb boils down to two possibilities. Either he was a stronger and more reasonable man than he is supposed to have been, and took at any rate an equal part in every decision about the upbringing of John; or he was so weak and unreasonable that Cynthia was forced to act unilaterally.

The first hypothesis means that both parents should be blamed or praised for what they did to John, Michael and Simon; the second introduces into the equation the extenuating factor of Cynthia's awareness of her inability to manage John as well as Beb, and still provide a fairly normal home life for Michael and Simon.

Cynthia's critics can see nothing good in the separation of John from the rest of his family. Yet I have observed families strained to breaking-point by the admirable resolve of wives and mothers to keep children like John at home: worn-out husbands and fathers at the end of their tether, brothers and sisters deeply disturbed by exposure to the sickness of their sibling who gets most of the attention. Far be it from me to slight the devotion and heroism of such women. I would nonetheless suggest that Michael and Simon may have been lucky not to be worried by or about John until they had reached the age of reason.

Some of the criticism has a financial and political basis: Lady Cynthia was able to buy her way out of trouble, she could afford private care for her son who could not eat scones like a little gentleman, she behaved as selfishly as most spoilt capitalists of her class – was she not the lucky one?

Setting aside the sneers of envy and dogma, Cynthia was caught in the trap, peculiarly painful, the effects of which elicit not much sympathy, which goes by the name of 'Keeping up appearances'. The scepticism of people from different walks of life notwithstanding, I wonder if it would have been possible not only psychologically, also physically, for her and for Beb to eke out their existence in the back of beyond. She was the daughter of an earl, the child of a stately home, the relation of powerful persons who would not permit her to sink into oblivion, and the popular friend – often the childhood friend – of persuasive hosts and hostesses insisting that they could not do without her. He was the son of a famous Prime Minister, he was again kept in his place by a thousand connections with the establishment, and a barrister by profession who needed to be in the metropolitan centre of things. And they were both Edwardians, born in the reign of Queen Victoria: society was strictly classified and stratified in their day.

They never did escape the circumstances of their birth and the consequential responsibilities. They felt they needed a decent home in a decent neighbourhood in which in decent attire sometimes to repay hospitality, and so on. Considering Beb's failure to win bread, Cynthia therefore earned money by playing poker, by doing literary hackwork and by submitting to Barrie, not merely to wallow in luxury, but to make ends meet, and especially to pay the price of John.

For how could John be protected from the health and strength of his brothers if they had to live together in the same smallish house, and how could his brothers be protected from John? How, if they were together, could he be stopped from mixing with their friends? How could he be educated differently, and treated in accordance with his disability?

At least exile for one brother, which was the more costly and organisationally complicated solution of the problem, spared the three of them much potential harm. John was sheltered from gossip, odious comparisons and publicity. Moreover he was not committed to an institution until he had reached the impossible age of puberty.

Cynthia, or Cynthia and Beb, or Cynthia and Beb and

all the doctors they consulted and all their advisers, may have erred, being human.

But I think no one should be arraigned for trying to do right, for struggling like Cynthia to do her best – more particularly because, in the opinion of many good people, the principle of what she did could not be bettered.

As for those figments of D. H. Lawrence's imagination, his descriptions of women which Mrs Beauman associates biographically with Cynthia: I would not presume to speak for so august a colleague as Lawrence, yet can say that I and fellow-novelists who are friends strongly object to readers insisting that our flights of fancy are nothing but slavish records and mere photographs of everyday life and real persons.

And I suspect that Lawrence, the man rather than the artist, would not like to be thought responsible for repeating that Cynthia was hard-hearted and unloving: it might be regarded as sour grapes – he might be classed with men who call women not responsive to their advances lesbians.

David Cecil fitted Lawrence into a literary pigeonhole under the heading Great Messes of Genius: Rousseau and Dostoevsky were also there. He meant that they were writers less restrained and refined than, for instance, Jane Austen or Turgenev. Lawrence in his letter to Cynthia insists that her attitude to John left room for improvement. But whether the outspoken childless author of *Lady Chatterley's Lover* fully appreciated her reticence, the delicacy of her emotions, and her proud refusal to betray her maternal anguish and burden others with it, is extremely dubious. David had minor faults to find with her mothering of Michael and Simon; but he knew her much longer than Lawrence did, he was born an aristocrat as she was, he too was a parent, and noted for his perspicacity and objectivity, and he never complained of her heartlessness. I cannot believe that Rachel and Leslie Hartley would have recognised her in the portraits in question in Lawrence's stories; I certainly do not.

Of course – and thank goodness – she was sophisticated: that is not to say she was shallow. She had been taught in a hard school the lesson of old Lady Salisbury that one must learn to laugh at nothing. Her good manners discouraged her from baring her soul. She did not parade her charity or advertise her worthiness.

Yet I can corroborate Leslie's tribute at her Memorial Service to the dependability of her friendship. I am sad to think of how much she must have suffered from being the mother – more than the friend – of John. And I hope my memories may have done her a little overdue justice.

RED LION HOUSE

RACHEL CECIL'S NOVEL *Theresa's Choice* was published in 1958. It was probably written at Linton Road, and after we became friends, although I have no recollection of her discussing it prior to publication. No doubt, and naturally enough as the wife of David, she was disinclined to broadcast news of her writing: she was apt to poke mocking fun at competitive wives trying to emulate their husbands – Countess Tolstoy, for example.

The 1958 literary scene differed from today's. Yet another sad thing about war is that it has a wonderful effect not only on weaponry, but also on the arts of peace: medicine, literature. Perhaps one ought to be happy that good should come out of evil, and that the plant of man's humanity needs to be watered with blood and tears.

War, at least, re-introduces the fashion for virtues such as courage, fortitude, unselfishness, generosity. Officer-like qualities and stiff upper lips are much in demand in wartime: not everybody is in favour of egalitarianism and equality of opportunity when it comes to dangerous missions, and nobody can be bothered with grousers and whiners. Accuracy is highly valued again: sloppy errors that cost lives are not smiled at and pardoned. The written word is therefore used with care. Writers, in order to account for dreadful events and experiences, once more hold the mirror up to nature and strive to tell the truth and find enlightenment in it. They are galvanised by horrid shocks to disseminate a counteractive and redemptive idealism.

Thirteen years after 1945, and the previous half a decade of savage fighting, quiet truthful books about nice responsible young heterosexual people looking for love and discovering happiness were still taken seriously.

Theresa's Choice startled the literary establishment nonetheless. It seemed out of date, pastiche Jane Austen, so direct as to be unsubtle, too naive to be true, and shamelessly middle-to-upper class. I must admit that I myself did not know quite what to make of it – I was taken aback by it being so un-'literary'. It employed none of the tricks of the trade; it was amateurish, yet so much the fresher; diffuse, yet polished; and neither low romantic fiction nor highly serious socio-sexual comedy – in short, it was unlike other books. Had Rachel, with her extensive knowledge of literature, tried to write a really novel form of novel? Had she failed? If so, would David have let her submit her work to public scrutiny?

I have recently re-read *Theresa's Choice* and revised my opinion. The contents had stuck in my mind for thirty years; and the book retains the distinction of being unlike others. It was a period piece when written – never 'modern' – and time has by now rendered it acceptably historical rather than dated. It is not so much naive as ingenuous, and its author does not suffer from the Uriah Heep-ishness of social guilt – she does not set her story in a class more inoffensively humble than the one she belongs to. It is individualistic; but I believe it records with fidelity the emotional facts of life for many young women. It is also funny and wise, and surely has at any rate one outstanding passage.

Theresa defends her engagement to get married thus: 'I don't think I'm too young. I am just twenty-one. I have been about since I was seventeen. It isn't very young to marry really, and I know it is the only thing I am fitted for ultimately.'

Having aired my grievance as a novelist against readers who identify fictional characters with real persons, I can hardly identify Theresa with Rachel herself.

But consistency is not natural; and my nature joins forces with my experience to convince me that Theresa's declaration – 'I know [marriage] is the only thing I am fitted for ultimately' – might have been made by Rachel. Indeed, I believe I can remember Rachel telling me something on the same lines, that she had always known it was her destiny to be a wife and mother.

Moreover, when all is said, *Theresa's Choice* is as autobiographical as most first novels. Theresa's romance with Edward Clare traces the course of Rachel's with David fairly closely.

The above is by no means to detract from the imaginative art of transforming fact into good fiction.

The story of the book is Theresa's love affair with 'wild' Ivor Brandon, then her agreement to marry Colin Evans, who has 'a dull name' and a character to match, and eventually the happy outcome of her hopes and plans in the shape of the proposal of 'extraordinary looking, almost bred away, but charming' Edward.

Theresa is sweet and diffident, but not so 'tame' as she supposes when comparing herself with Ivor: she writes letters to Colin Evans and to Edward Clare that lead on to her receiving offers of marriage from both men. And she firmly turns down Ivor's propositions.

Ivor Brandon, whose name is evocative and not dull, exemplifies a type of person that never ceased to fascinate David and Rachel. He is not just a minor Don Juan, spoilt by women, disorganised, demanding and vaguely desperate. Edward Clare answers thus, when Theresa asks what he thinks of Ivor: 'He has got so many qualities that I like: humour – passion – temperament for life – recklessness – taste . . . I have known other people who are like him – women too. They are often passionate and feel strongly, and one can't say they haven't any heart exactly, yet they aren't quite human . . . They react in a way which would not seem odd in a child; but which is odd in a grown-up. I have heard them described as leprechauns.'

Edward continues: 'I should say he was too selfish [to be lovable] . . . He's not intellectual, but sensual. He goes entirely by his feelings, and he is inarticulate when it comes to intimacy . . . Perhaps [leprechauns] dimly realise there is something different about themselves. But they never think of themselves any more than animals do. They are egotistic in the way that an animal is.'

Theresa asks elsewhere in the book if Ivor is neurotic.

Edward replies: 'I shouldn't wonder. Nearly everyone is. But I don't think true leprechauns are . . . There are no rules . . . But once you see [the point about leprechauns], it is like having the key to a puzzle.'

Edward Clare is not only charming, and interestingly analytical of 'leprechauns', he is also unintentionally comical and the cause of comedy in others. I refer particularly to the episode which begins: 'Poor Edward! Did you hear him crash on the stairs?' He and Theresa are fellow-guests at a weekend party in a country house, and he has 'charged down [stairs] in the usual way', missed his footing and sprained his ankle. Somebody says that he 'feels shock very badly', and somebody else remembers 'when Lady Morpeth shut [his] finger in the door of the motor at Horton. He behaved like Mrs Disraeli, but how he paid for it after . . . He was ill for about a fortnight.' The hostess, Lady Sybil, comments: '"I know, he's not strong," glancing sympathetically at Theresa,' who has fallen in love with Edward and hopes to marry him. The doctor arrives to look at the ankle, and the conversation of the gentry includes the following exchange: 'It's not long ago that [Edward] had another fall . . .' 'Yes, he's always falling down.' Then Theresa goes to visit the man she loves, who is in bed and looking 'very pale and fragile propped up with pillows'. He confesses: 'I expect my shoelace was undone – I have weak ankles too.' He does not spare her the rather humiliating details of his reaction to the accident: 'I suffered terribly from shock at the time. My teeth were chattering for about a quarter of an hour . . . Have you ever had it? The doctor said it was a rigor.' Her humorously tart response is conclusive: 'No. I thought only dogs had it – or there's rigor mortis – at least it wasn't that!'

When the course of Theresa's love for Edward does not run smooth, and he has apparently taken fright and evasive action, she writes him a letter. It is again un-literary, stylistically just the sort of inconsequential stuff a girl of Theresa's age, in Theresa's position, might pour out. At the same time it is extraordinarily sensitive, tactful, intelligent, persuasive and touching; and it seems to me the best thing in the book, and outstanding by any standards.

Here are a few of its sentences: 'I have felt lately that you may have been wondering what I feel, and that you may not have wanted to come and see me so often . . . That is why I am struggling to say all this, as I do feel it would be the greatest pity if our friendship got spoilt – I would really mind that . . . It might be so easy to drift apart. I am very devoted to you, but I have always felt that you were more suited to friendships than to emotional relationships – and that is why it is so delightful talking to you, and being with you . . . If you know this it may be easier for you when we next meet. I can't bear to think that you may have worried . . .'

A comparison of this letter with that written by Push-kin's Tatyana to Eugene Onegin, and of the respective results, springs to mind. Women with romantic and matrimonial intentions would do well to study it. Tatyana declared her passion for Onegin, and was offered with disdain scarcely more than a brother's love; whereas Theresa offered Edward Clare the freedom of a sister's love, which provoked him to propose to marry her.

Edward's description of how he came to pop the question might have cooled the ardour of some women: 'I even took my temperature in the train, I felt so queer . . . Directly I heard your voice in the garden I knew that

I had to propose.' But Theresa is so happy 'that she wanted to shout and dance like a child'.

She leaves Ivor Brandon in the lurch, and has no thoughts to spare for Colin Evans. She excuses herself with two neat aphorisms: 'Nothing is so heartless as love. Nobody behaves well.'

And she generalises the explanation of her love of Edward: 'Perhaps it is what most women want – to be understood and share the same point of view . . . When they *do* find someone who really sympathises and feels like they do, it's that which satisfies them – not physical attraction, or even simple goodness and dependability.'

The author of *Theresa's Choice* was naive neither in real life, nor on paper, except superficially.

She must have shown me a page or two of the typescript of the book or of something else she had written, where she called mildly flirtatious chat 'making love' – as in the following example invented by me: She handed him his hat and gloves in the hall while he made love to her. But Rachel was merely using the jargon of her youth rather than of mine, and had not caught up with the fact that the making of love means sexual intercourse in the age of permissiveness.

Whether or not she knew more than she wrote about the 'Cadmans', whom she herself identified with Eric Gill and his family, is and will probably remain an open question. Theresa's visit to the homespun religious community in the country is observed amusingly: the sandals and woven ties worn by the men, the head-scarves and specs of the four Cadman daughters, Zillah, Gwyneth, Phoebe and Demeter, the vegetarian lunch and icy rooms and compline at three o'clock. Theresa decides that Daniel Cadman, artist and paterfamilias, is 'quite unnoticing of women', and that the girls' bedrooms are 'like nuns' cells'. Was Rachel being discreet? Had she no inkling that, as we have now been told, Eric Gill was an absolute satyr, copulating with any woman he could get hold of, including his daughters?

But if she failed to detect the bizarre goings-on in the Cadman-Gill household, in that unlikely event she is just exhibiting the minor defect of a major quality of her novel, which does not err and stray beyond the range of its author's experience. In these unisex days, women writers are inclined to think they can impersonate men, and vice versa.

Theresa's Choice has the ring of truth throughout, and its heroine gradually casts a gentle spell over the reader.

RACHEL TALKED ABOUT a second book. Its hero, or central figure, was to be a nobleman, a baronet or baron; and I believe she started to write it. But then she told me that she wished, she had decided, to publish nothing else. The reason she gave was that she did not like the limelight.

But in some roundabout way I heard that a by-product of the publication of *Theresa's Choice* was a request for an interview from a well-known female journalist. Rachel granted the interview, entertained the journalist to tea, rather enjoyed her company and talked to her fairly freely. In due course a vicious sneering feature appeared in a newspaper: which put Rachel off the whole business of writing books and becoming fair game for cannibalistic journalism in consequence.

Later on she must have regretted her decision to discontinue that second book. She spoke nostalgically of the spare time she had had at Linton Road, thanks to her staff and in spite of her children: it had enabled her to write *Theresa's Choice*, and the lack of it thereafter rendered her incapable of the sustained concentration and effort of authorship.

She had been younger and stronger, too, at Linton Road. As a hostess she always showed stamina, and her active concern for everyone did not falter or fail. Yet she remarked on more than one occasion that life was simply a battle against tiredness.

Removal from Linton Road meant a double move into Charlbury Road in Oxford and Red Lion House in Cranborne. Bereavement, divorce and moving house are acknowledged by medical experts to be the most traumatic experiences of life, apart from illness; and Rachel might have wished to insert in that list not only moving into two considerable houses almost simultaneously, but running them.

Her situation below stairs, metaphorically speaking, for in fact she never had a house with a basement, deteriorated. She began to suffer from that inescapable ailment reserved for top people: the servant problem. The migration of her household from Oxford to Cranborne in university vacations, and back again in term-times, doubtless frayed even further the typically ragged nervous systems of cooks. But Rachel's cooks continued to cause consternation after Charlbury Road was sold, and roots and toes were dug in at Red Lion House.

Perhaps the Cecils did not or could not pay the going rate for the job. A more surprising explanation of the trouble in the Cecils' kitchens may be that David, and Rachel herself, were not all that easy to work for. Let me hasten to add that they were never unkind to anyone, and seemed to me to spoil their staff. But David carried absent-mindedness to extremes: he was so absent-minded that once at a luncheon party I saw him put on his plate a whole steamed pudding – he was the first of the five or six guests to be offered it. He had been brought up in the grandest style, he took domestic service for granted, and his impersonal attitude possibly and mistakenly looked like snootiness from a servant's point of view. I cannot imagine him congratulating a cook on her cooking, for example, since he was completely uninterested in and unaware of what he ate.

Rachel, on the other hand, may have gone wrong for the opposite reason. Neither emotionally nor materially had she had so secure a childhood as David. Her parents' marriage was not happy ever after, her father was susceptible to feminine charm, her mother was slowly immured in deafness, and money was in short supply. The strain of keeping up appearances would have affected her through no fault of her own, sooner, at an earlier age, and therefore more disturbingly than it affected Cynthia. She may have had to act as her mother's intermediary with staff. The servants of poor or sick employers, think-

ing they are or knowing they are thought to be indispensable, have a tendency to try a bit of blackmail: was
Rachel's girlhood frightened by threats of that sort? Was
she humiliated by having to beg for help – and so inhibited
for the rest of her life in her dealings with professional
helpers?

She had a phobia about housework, cooking especially.
The origin of it could have been the dread of having to
shop and cook and clean for her mother, and of finding
herself on the slippery slope of social demotion. Women
with more privileged backgrounds than hers, and men
too, have learned belatedly and enthusiastically to look
after themselves and their families. Rachel was almost
paralysed with horror at the prospect. She could not
contemplate with equanimity even the possibility of
muddling through. Thus, in the terms of industrial relations, she must have negotiated with employees from a
position of weakness.

Yet another question occurs to me: did intimate influ-
ences also sap her strength? Her marriage to David was
romantic not least because it included the element of
rescue: he had rescued her from the possible fate of
becoming a poor drudge – he had appeared with a Ladder
when circumstances were nudging her towards a Snake.
Did she feel bound by gratitude, honour and love to
maintain certain standards in his homes, and at least
provide four decent meals a day without subjecting him
to her hopeless cookery?

Setting aside unanswerable hypotheses, the difficulties
encountered by Rachel on the domestic front in the
post-Linton Road era probably boiled down to the

numbers she had to cater for. There were five in the family, eight and more when the three children married and grandchildren appeared on the scene; and relations and friends and people connected with David's work were invited to stay and for meals.

And Rachel's resigned remark is a summing-up: 'All women are bad with servants.'

The above is very far from suggesting that she was lazy or incompetent. On the contrary – that she would not and could not cook is worthy of record only because she was otherwise so competent and willing. She was such a handy electrician that I nicknamed her 'Sparks'; and she bustled about constructively and nearly always provided or presided over the edible goods. And her complaints were exceptional and muted.

Besides, she never complained in my hearing of having to shoulder more organisational responsibilities than the majority of wives: I think it never, or no longer, crossed her mind to object to paying the bills, managing the family finances, dealing with workmen, and so on. David, apparently, confined his practical assistance to making essential telephone calls – he liked and she loathed to speak on the telephone; to putting in position in their sitting-rooms the little tables on which she laid the tea things; and to pulling the occasional cork out of a bottle of wine. Sometimes he also drove the car – but that was against her will.

She was 'fitted for' marriage – and she seemed to excel at it; and marital loyalty together with experience of authorship would have encouraged her to protect her husband's writing. No doubt, too, considering his clumsiness, prudence advised her not to let him carry trays of china teacups or even help himself to meat, veg and gravy from the sideboard. And she had reason to fear that he would forget to pay for electricity or water.

It was still generous of her to relieve him of so many duties and chores. I suspect that he would have been capable of doing everything she did for him, although he might not have bothered to. But he did not hesitate, he was happy, to delegate: he had a marked gift for hands-off delegation. Perhaps, in their early married days, she had uttered those four seductive words, 'Leave it to me,' taking pity on his worried vagueness. As a result the David I knew had developed into quite a cosseted pasha in his home life.

The virtue that redeemed his acceptance of her tireless activity on his behalf was the sweetness of his temper. He asked for nothing, he criticised nothing, he was unendingly appreciative and grateful; and he surely would have done his share with a good grace, if she had not felt it would be quicker, more effective and less trouble to do it herself. Surely, again, he was ever ready to discuss the doing, and to put at her disposal his calm rationality.

After all, love loves to serve the beloved: David as well as Rachel acted out this truism in different ways.

My introduction to the domestic strife, that is the strife with domestics, which they both suffered from, was their humorous account of a crisis at Charlbury Road. They had employed a married couple from Spain: the wife who cooked was overweight, the husband who served at table and did odd jobs was squat, hirsute, cheerful and kind. David and Rachel liked him very much, notwithstanding the difficulty of communication since he had no English. One day two policemen came to talk to David about his manservant, who had formed the bad habit of exposing himself to the young pupils walking home in the afternoon from a nearby girls' school. Complaints had been received from the girls' parents; proof had been obtained that the man committed the offence regularly standing at David's garden gate. He was summoned and accused – he understood not a word. David had to telephone and ask the Oxford Professor of Spanish to come and interpret. Everyone was embarrassed. The luckier end of the affair was that the police decided not to press charges, provided the culprit returned to Spain forthwith. The unluckier end was that the Cecils were once more servantless.

RED LION HOUSE, so-called because it had been a sometime pub of that name, stands a few feet back from the narrow pavement and the road running through Cranborne, which nestles below the high sweep of Cranborne Chase, on the lower slopes of Pentridge Hill, and in the very heart of Hardy's Wessex. The village is or was rustically picturesque and agricultural, although it can boast two small stately homes, Cranborne Manor and Cranborne Lodge. It has a shop or two and a garage, a Garden Centre, and a clear stream in which watercress used to be and may still be grown.

The red of Red Lion House may have referred to the

brick it was built of. As I remember, part of it was old, but additions had been tacked on in this century. It had a spacious hall with staircase and an extension like a miniature conservatory into the garden at the back of the house; sitting-room, dining-room and large study for David; and domestic offices including some of the cook's quarters, all on the ground floor. On the first floor were five bedrooms, plus more accommodation for the cook, and on the attic floor an unknown number of attic bedrooms. I always used the only bathroom on the first floor: David and Rachel would vacate it for guests and use the other one, surprisingly situated downstairs and next to the study. Another surprise, at least for me, was the barn-like storeroom reached through the study: I discovered or was shown it after countless visits to the house.

The sitting-room was painted strong apple-green, and again, as at Linton Road, had the fine French desk in a corner. The portrait of Peniston Lamb, dashing and dandified, who died young, hung above the drinks tray: he was the elder brother of William, Lord Melbourne, the subject of David's biography. In the yellow hall was the portrait by Anthony Devas of Rachel in youth under a parasol. An upright piano, its wood bleached by sunlight, and the desk piled with bills and papers for Rachel to sort out, stood in the south-facing windowed extension. A solid fuel Pither stove, fixed in the fireplace, heated the hall in winter. The bedrooms were just nicely comfortable, without being at all luxurious. As usual, there were books everywhere.

Out in the road, a little farther from the village, was

an entrance in a high wall to the backyard of Red Lion House, probably a stableyard of yore. The Cecils kept their car here in a proper old barn, as proved not only by the vehicle itself, but also by the damage done to the wooden gates and gateposts set in the wall and to the barn doors: Rachel did not always succeed in discouraging David from driving in and out. Once she got into the car in the barn and was starting it, when a tramp who had been sleeping in the back seat reared his ugly head and confronted her in the driving-mirror.

The garden could be reached from the yard. Mainly, access was by way of a partly glazed door in the rear hall of the house, where coats and gumboots dwelt. Some very occasional gardener must have mown the lawn and tidied up, for the garden was not totally unkempt, and it had a careless charm. The ground behind the house rose sharply to that lawn – you had to mount steps in order to be on the level, where we played croquet. Spring bulbs in rough grass, a hedge of overgrown shrubs, lichened fruit trees and a few tilled beds provided the horticultural interest. David always seemed able to find enough flowers to put in vases – he had a gift for arranging cut flowers: he relieved Rachel of this obligation of gracious living, too.

A wall on the left separated their garden from that of their friendly neighbour, a doctor who rejoiced in the same name as the art historian Kenneth Clark. And a secret door in the wall at the back opened into land owned and cultivated by the Cecil family for centuries. Beyond and parallel to the back wall, and rising far above it, was the avenue of Cornish elm trees, dark-foliaged, rook-favoured, two or three hundred yards long, which had once flanked a driveway to Cranborne Manor – cows now grazed and chewed the cud in their shade.

I think Bobbety Salisbury's son Robert – Robert and Mollie Cranborne and their numerous offspring – had already taken up residence at the Manor by the time David and Rachel moved into Red Lion House.

However, David was not the only Cecil to yield to the magnetic attractions of the place. For elder sons of the Marquesses of Salisbury, traditional occupants of Cranborne Manor while their fathers reigned over Hatfield House, it was usually the scene of nuptial bliss as well as happy childhood. Bobbety, who had been Viscount Cranborne not long before, was a case in point. He and his wife Betty had lived at the Manor for years and loved it, had raised three sons and mourned two of them there, had made a splendid garden and generally sunk roots. When he inherited the title and they needed to remove to Hatfield, they maintained their connection with Cranborne by spending any spare time they had at the Lodge, possibly built for that very purpose. It was just across the road from the Manor and a few hundred yards from Red Lion House.

David with his strong family feelings was pleased to be able to see his busy brother sometimes, and, with his understanding of and sympathy for youth, to keep in touch with his younger relations. He liked the idea of the continuity of being at Cranborne again; and Rachel shared his sentimental attachment to the area, since Rockbourne and the house where they had spent their early married life pre-war were just five miles away. They were both appreciative of the beauty of the Dorset countryside, and rightly persuaded that they were providing their children with the best of all possible homes.

A bonus was the arrival of Anne Tree in a village within visiting distance. The Trees had had to sell Mereworth Castle, and had moved into a smaller house in the Shaftesbury direction. They wanted to see as much as they could of the Cecils, and vice versa. And then Anne invited her mother, who was David's sister Moucher, to stay, and her own sister Elizabeth Cavendish, another of David's much-loved nieces.

I USED TO TAKE the train to Salisbury and be met by David or Rachel or both. Rachel was inclined to drive straight home, David to meander, looking too often at his passenger and pointing out sights, via Rockbourne or the woods of Martin, in which Tess of the d'Urbervilles is supposed to have been seduced.

Quite often I was their only guest. Since each of them liked a duologue, I was therefore asked into David's study for chats, then taken for walks by Rachel. One visit was meant to restore me to health and happiness after glandular fever; unfortunately I could not bring myself to swallow a mouthful of food at meals, but became ravenously hungry at other times and had to beg Rachel for digestive biscuits.

Incidentally, Rachel was a biscuit-fancier, she knew

biscuits backwards, and introduced Cynthia and me to Dad's Cookies, for which we developed a craze.

On another occasion I gave the Cecils a glimpse of that horror of hospitality, the unwell guest. But luckily my indispositions were slight, and certainly nothing to do with staying at Red Lion House, tiring as I found it to talk so much, to have to think so much, in the company of my host and hostess. In fact their company, because it was such fun as well as stimulating and edifying, always in the end had a tonic effect.

Although I greatly enjoyed our threesomes, and basking in the full attention of the Cecils, I think that in principle they preferred foursomes. The tried and tested idea that equal numbers of men and women make the best social mix cannot be improved upon; and it really is easier for two people to walk and talk together than for three. Moreover, from my point of view, an extra nice thing about the Cecils was that they had nice friends.

Sometimes one of David's sisters, Mima Harlech or Moucher Devonshire, was my fellow-guest for weekends. Moucher's widowhood was fully occupied: she had become Mistress of the Robes to the Queen, and Chancellor of Exeter University, and was knee-deep in good causes. The passage of time had changed but not detracted from her beauty, nor dulled the eager sympathy of her responses: she still charmed me as she had at Churchdale Hall in Derbyshire long ago. David was also an admirer of her looks and manners; and because he was so extraordinarily objective, his admiration was not mere fraternal loyalty, but probably representative of masculine and indeed intersexual opinion. He had a memory of her waltzing at a ball when she was young and unmarried, and he used to say that she had come closest to his idea of Natasha in glorious youth in *War and Peace*. I could see what he meant – imagine the similarity – notwithstanding my guess that Natasha would have been more headstrong and sensual.

For Mima and Moucher too, Cranborne was the home of their childhood. We would be sure to go to the Manor if one of them was staying at Red Lion House, perhaps by way of the door in the garden wall and the old drive under the elms, or via the downhill slope of the village street and the churchyard.

And I have a picture in my mind's eye of Moucher at this period – Moucher and David strolling together across the spreading lawns and through the flowery enclosures of the Manor gardens. Mollie and their nephew Robert and their five great-nephews and their great-niece must have been absent, for they are alone, walking ahead of Rachel and me; and the scene seems to be autumnal, although that part of my recollection might be too symbolic to be true. The romantic aspect of the grey-haired figures of brother and sister has become historical – more to do with history than with their personal appearances: for they are descended from three great Prime Ministers, they have added honours to the uniquely long record of the Cecil family's excellence and eminence, and they are on ground given to their forebear for services rendered to the nation four hundred years previously.

Anne Tree would ask us over to her home for dinner on the Saturday evening of weekends, or David and Rachel asked neighbours in to dine. They were hospitality itself so far as I was concerned; but I know that some people categorised them as guests by vocation rather than as hosts. Since they were so popular and socially in demand, they may have been more accustomed to and practised in the former role. Again, they may have felt shy about inviting friends used to a high standard of living to share their always adequate, but humbler, repasts.

Their strict rationing of social activities of all sorts was an unmixed blessing for their own visitors. At any rate I was thankful not to be rushed around the countryside and introduced to scores of strangers at weekends. Invitations poured in: David often had to charge out of the sitting-room, across the hall and into the lobby outside his study in order to answer the telephone and stem the flow. In spite of his repeated claim that he was going to die of politeness, he could be blunt if his graceful hints were not taken. To those who tried to badger and corner him and force the issue, he was capable of saying: 'The fact of the matter is that we don't want to come to your house.' And he bravely barred the door against weekenders in big houses in the neighbourhood who otherwise would have been brought over and loosed upon us.

One person who as it were battered down David's defences was Cecil Beaton. Cecil's country home at Broad Chalke in Wiltshire was not far away, he would insist on calling, and he even persuaded David to visit his studio and sit to have a portrait painted.

Cecil was a very smart man in every sense. He put turn-ups on the cuffs of the jackets of his suits, and lapels on his waistcoats – he either created fashions or was the first to follow them. He wore cream-coloured flannels in summer in the country, and was seldom without a fancy-dress-type of hat on his head – his hats were rather becoming. He brilliantly bridged the gulf between hetero-sexuality and homosexuality, taking full advantage of the favour of the 'Homintern' on the one hand, and publicly protesting that he was at least a soul-brother of lovers of women on the other. He had a great talent for photo-graphy, which is much rarer than today's superfluity of over-praised and over-exposed photographers may suggest; and, by dint of the hardest work and relentless publicity-seeking, he managed to convince the world that he was also a top-class designer of book-jackets and theatrical sets and costumes, painter, writer and diarist.

He had regular features and a tall elegant figure. He looked like an actor trying to look like a retired ambassador or a gentleman of the old school. His eyes were alarming, sharp, piercing, cold, sceptical – they reminded me of loaded pistols; and his hungry smile startled. His humour was the catty kind, and he carried on long-running obses-sive vendettas against real or imaginary enemies. As a somewhat effeminate youth, at a ball given by the Pem-brokes of Wilton, he was thrown in the lake by a gang of gilded contemporaries, but he clambered out, and back to the ball, and up and up the social ladder: his passport throughout his successful life was his courage.

David Cecil and Cecil Beaton, who had known each other for years, remained more acquaintances than friends. David made mock of the variety of hats worn by Cecil partly to cover his baldness, and disapproved of his shabby treatment of Greta Garbo: Cecil gained access into her closely guarded privacy, became her friend, even her lover in his own estimation, then told the whole story in his published diary. But David was quite amused to hear the latest gossip from Cecil, and intrigued by his passion for success, which stopped at nothing.

Why did Cecil seek out David? They had little in common: for Cecil did not see David's jokes, was not as literary as all that, and shared none of his unworldly values. Perhaps he was clever enough to recognise and admire a superior person; and, like the rest of us, derived benefit from being in David's and Rachel's presence.

Summer at Red Lion House was sunshine flooding in through the windows at the back; country sounds of birds' wooing, insects toiling, a tractor, cows; tea on the croquet lawn and long light evenings. The proximity of the road somehow accentuated the remoteness of the village: cars passed in the balmy night, but so rarely as to prove we were in the middle of nowhere, and horses trotted echoingly through the mists of morning.

But one particular time of day at Red Lion House in winter keeps coming back to me: the post-prandial hours. Having dined we would return to the sitting-room and the fire would be made up. The room got hotter – David or Rachel piled more coal and a log on it – they were apparently impervious to the rising temperature. I roasted and sweated, and laughed and learned, and realised how lucky I was to be there.

At length we adjourned to the bedroom floor and David's rigmarole with books began, while Rachel fiddled with her electrical appliances, night-storage heaters or electric blankets threateningly old. It was sad that our day, or weekend together, was ending, but a slight compensatory relief to be cooler – I speak for myself. Had I read this book, would I like to read that one, David asked, adding to the pile of reading matter on my bedside table. Rachel was sure that if I could stand the intermittent ticking of the old electric blanket it would keep me warm and not kill me.

We said good night and sleep well. But sleep was out of the question for the next half-hour or so, especially when Jonathan or Hugh or Laura, or all three, happened to be at home. The members of the family would all call to one another, and loudly ascend and descend stairs, and slam doors: it was like listening to a recording of wild creatures which were at their most active round about midnight, or a composition satirising the musical avant-garde by Hoffnung. Somebody thundered down to the bathroom on the ground floor, slamming through the swing-doors, slamming the bathroom door twice, slamming back through the swing-doors, and thundering up again. Somebody else was slamming doors on the attic floor. There was continual jolly talk and laughter, punctuated by the calling of names and the fullstops of more doors slammed.

Peace broke out finally. Yet the house was seldom, if ever, completely quiet in my experience. David and Rachel were still talking, I could hear his high and low voice and cackling laugh and the ready twitter of her rejoinders, as I dropped off; and the same applied to my waking.

BOOKS AND LETTERS

WHEN DAVID RETIRED from his professorship of English Literature at Oxford, he and Rachel sold Charlbury Road as planned and settled permanently at Red Lion House.

His biography of Max Beerbohm, *Max*, was published in 1964. Did he write it at Cranborne? Had he severed his connection with Oxford by the time it appeared?

The precise answers to such questions are irrelevant in an impressionistic memoir such as I am trying to write. Suffice it to say that I believe the mysterious illness of some months' duration, the scientific cause of which was identified with difficulty as Germ Q, struck David down at Red Lion House and as a result of the marathon of his eight years of hard labour on *Max*.

He loved Max's work, and was proud to know that Max had wanted him to do the biography. But although he wrote in his Prefatory Note, 'Max's life was so uneventful that it is almost impossible to make a story of it' – a sentence and a sentiment equally applicable to David's own life – he had to cope with a mass of material and ended up with a very long book: two hundred and fifty thousand words approximately. The effort involved in controlling a monster of that size, remembering what you have and have not said, keeping your commitment alive and refreshing and reviving it year in and year out, preserving your sense of proportion and your confidence, and maintaining the momentum of composition, not to mention standards and quality, has made many an author ill: some people wonder if Tolstoy ever recovered from the seven years of his work on *War and Peace*.

That David did recover from the achievement of *Max*, and vanquished Germ Q, testifies to the strength of his mind and his constitution. He was living proof of the health-giving effects of a childhood and youth spent more in bed than in schoolrooms and on playing-fields, and, probably, of having stopped smoking cigarettes. So far as I know, with the exception of Germ Q, he had no serious adult setback either physical or mental. And *Max* was his ninth book; he was a leading light of Oxford University, and lectured to full houses; he was a happy husband with a happy wife, and a devoted father of his children; and he was a social lion with a host of close friends and the widest possible circle of acquaintances.

Of course he had vitality. Mental events obviously crowded in on him, and he seemed not to get too tired. And because he talked so much, so fast and in such a carrying voice, his vocal apparatus must have been made of steel and leather.

But his physique was hardly herculean. Where did he get the requisite energy to supply the demands of his varied interests? How did he find the time?

He told me that he liked to write, and often wrote best, at night – after dinner and until the small hours of the morning. I half-remember him telling me that at least once he was inspired to write the whole night through. Yet he was not noticeably an owl rather than a lark – he had his wits about him all day; and burning the candle at both ends surely would or should have been counter-productive in the longer run.

He was fascinated by the methods of other writers, not just Joyce Cary's, and discoursed amusingly on the subject: Thomas Hardy having to smell an apple he kept in his desk before he was able to start writing; Tennyson repeatedly signing his name; Chekhov putting on his best clothes and Kuprin stripping off his clothes; and Schiller submerging his bare feet in a basin of cold water. Apparently Byron was also a nocturnal scribe: he would go to dinner parties, come home, drink brandy and then versify. I cannot believe that David wrote after parties, and he would not have had recourse to alcohol.

His spidery longhand was rendered no more legible by his habit of going over certain words and letters with his pen. And he ruthlessly crossed out, inserted and transposed – I cannot suppress a pang of sympathy for the secretary who typed that Lord Melbourne ended his days in tranquil obscenity.

The English he wrote has that indescribable quality, style. It is accurate and clear, it fudges no issue, it has authority and pace, it leaves an impression of light and warmth, and the author seems to speak to the reader in a quiet charming voice. At the same time what he put on paper was a mixture of scrupulousness and nonchalance: he undoubtedly took infinite care to say what he meant and to get his historical facts as right as possible, yet he did not allow pedantry or barren perfectionism to stand in his way.

The sentence in *Lord M.* describing Mrs Norton, if I may repeat it, illustrates the above: 'He was ushered up into a minute drawing-room, bright with flowers and muslin curtains and almost filled by a large blue sofa, from which rose to greet him a young woman of glittering beauty – all opulent shoulder and raven's wing hair, who bending forward a little, looked up at him meltingly from under sweeping lashes and whose blood, as she spoke, mantled delicately under a clear olive skin.' David here uses two 'ups' and two 'unders'. His 'from which' in the context, and his 'and whose', are ugly and awkward constructions, and his punctuation is peculiar.

I am reminded of the short essay by David I was once called upon to edit. The typescript he sent me was quite a mess, and I had to ask his permission to rearrange and re-punctuate it. He gave me a free hand and did not object to the changes I had made – he probably could not be bothered to check them.

He loved our language, its richness and infinite ambiguity, constituting grist to the mill of poetry and the best prose. But his attitude to writing it was grand and old-fashioned, Elizabethan almost: he demonstrated that he was its master, never its slave, and he regarded it as the mere means to the end of re-creating life. He was out to set the scene, to resurrect the persons of the drama, and, above all, to convey feeling, their feelings and his own. I can vouch for his success inasmuch as I have remembered for forty years his account of Lord Melbourne meeting Mrs Norton, which he read aloud to the party at Compton Place; and because my memory is of the disillusioned aristocratic politician and the beautiful ambitious younger woman, not of David's grammar.

Considering that his literary concern was life rather than history, if such a distinction can be made, or, to put it in other ways, why as well as how things happened, the psychology of events, also the morality, he might have become a novelist – he seemed to be equipped to. But he wrote, or published, no fiction. His academic studies and critical analyses of the fictional form possibly had some sort of inhibiting effect. I often urged him to write his recollections of interesting friends and acquaintances, if not his autobiography. He said he could not tell the truth about people either living or recently dead. For similar reasons, possibly again, he shrank from the ineluctable fate of the novelist, which is to have his or her inventions even libellously confused with reality. Anyway, he was called to be a biographer, and his biographies are works of imagination.

They are still much read; and readers of them will draw their own conclusions. I would not presume to judge David's work. Yet I must admit that I was surprised on re-reading *Melbourne* not long ago: *Melbourne* being the unification of *The Young Melbourne* and *Lord M*. On the second page of the first chapter the author begins to dissect the character of Lady Melbourne, the mother of the subject of the book. He catalogues her accomplishments and her qualities, then introduces the list of her defects thus: 'All the same it is impossible to approve of Lady Melbourne. Her outlook was both low and limited. To her the great world of rank and fashion was the only world; and she saw it as a battle ground in which most people fought for their own ends. Nor was hers an amiable cynicism. She was good-tempered, not good-natured; suave, but not soft. Her laughter was satirical and unfeeling, she could not resist a wounding thrust. And, on the rare occasions she judged it wise to lose her temper, she was both relentless and brutal.'

The shock for me was the forthright and confident disapproval. David is assuming that behaviour can by common consent be measured by how far it rises above or falls below some golden mean – presumably the Christian ethic or a widely agreed standard of decency. In my opinion his moral stance is fully justified in principle, and by the reasoning with which he backs it up.

But what he did is done no longer. *The Young Melbourne* was first published in 1939, and *Lord M.* in 1954 – in other words, before the age of permissiveness, which put the finishing touch to what was left of the moral consensus. Writers now take care not to discriminate illiberally between virtue and vice, and publishers are against uncommercial puritanism: few exceptions prove those rules.

Although David's definition of art did not altogether satisfy the absolutism of my youth, increasingly it appeals to me. It can be summed up in a single word: delight – he was too canny to box himself in with an elaborate and rigid formula. Clearly, would-be art that never delights anyone is not art; while the criterion of delightfulness can be applied by different people to works of art of every type and description. It may smack of the ridiculed platitude: 'I don't know much about art, but I do know what I like.' Yet, after all, that platitude is the bedrock of aesthetics; and David particularised within the broad sweep of his generalisation, as indicated by his literary likes and dislikes.

I WOULD SAY that his ideal novelists were Jane Austen and Ivan Turgenev. The former lived through the French Revolution and the Napoleonic Wars, but she ignored them in her novels; nevertheless David in his biography of her denied that she was an escapist, and I can deny that he was one. Admittedly he preferred not to be assaulted and upset by the crude sex and savagery and other horrors of the so-called 'communications industry' of his latter years; and, like his fellow-historians and most artists, he was attracted by the romance and dignity of the past. However, he compared Jane Austen with Mozart, and considered that the greatness of their genius took into account the whole human condition; and he read and marvelled at Turgenev's essay entitled *The Execution of Tropmann*, which is awfully grisly.

Turgenev's essay is his eye-witness record of the last hours and the public guillotining in Paris of the child-murderer Tropmann. It is fraught with terror and pity, and pleads for the abolition either of capital punishment or public executions. David did not shy away from it. Although he cannot have liked the subject, he would have equated the thrill of reading that writing, which is wonderful even in translation, with 'delight'; and he had no objections to the sensationalism, since the story is true, told with absolute objectivity, and to illustrate an humane theme.

Flaubert, on the other hand, was disliked because he was a 'cruel' writer and gloried in cruelty for its own sake. David took exception to the surgical details in *Madame Bovary*, and loathed the bloodbath of *Salammbô*; and he did not altogether share my partiality for *L'Education Sentimentale*. He had no romantic illusions about the characters of writers, but believed that any marked abnormality of an artist's psyche – a sadistic tendency, for example – was sooner or later destructive of his or her art. He was dismissive of Richard Hughes because, in *A High Wind in Jamaica*, the description of a man drowning concludes with words to this effect: 'and his death was slow, because he was a strong swimmer.' David's view was that the only purpose of the conclusion was to give pleasure to the author and pain to the reader.

He was not at ease with French literature in general. In a rather John Bull-ish way he thought Flaubert's obsession with style pernickety and precious – unstylish, in fact. He had praise for Proust as a comic writer, but said the filial love in *A La Recherche* was a bit too hothouse, the adult loves were about jealousy, not really about love at all, and the book in twelve English volumes was on the long side. He suggested that homosexual writers had special difficulties in so controlling and adapting their attitudes as to create any complete work of art by the heterosexual standards presently in force.

Of the works of Turgenev, he especially loved *A Sports-*

man's *Sketches*, *Fathers and Sons*, and *Smoke*. The gentleness and pliability of Turgenev, who, strangely enough, was regarded as a controversialist in Russia in his lifetime, appealed to him slightly more than the strength of Tolstoy. Yet he also loved Tolstoy's writing, including the books and stories of Tolstoy's extreme old age, the first half of *Resurrection*, for instance, and *The Death of Ivan Ilyich* and *Father Sergius*. Chekhov was his favourite playwright after Shakespeare, and *The Three Sisters* his favourite Chekhov play. He admired books by less famous nineteenth-century Russian writers, Lermontov's *A Hero of our Time*, Goncharov's *The Same Old Story*; and then *Dr Zhivago* and Solzhenitsyn's *Cancer Ward*.

But David's very own territory was Eng. Lit. His *Early Victorian Novelists* and *Hardy The Novelist* are often said to be the best things he ever did. I remember his references to three books that made deep impressions on him: *Alice in Wonderland* when he was a child; and in young adulthood Lytton Strachey's *Eminent Victorians* and Virginia Woolf's *To the Lighthouse*.

He was more reliable as critical assessor of dead novelists than of living or contemporary ones: I have to say it in spite of being a beneficiary of the criticism he wrote for newspapers. He was not that great rarity, the born critic, like the Russian Belinsky, or his father-in-law Desmond MacCarthy. He was more like those artist – writers who have been notoriously bad at picking literary winners and losers: Tolstoy who said that Chekhov could not write plays, and Henry James who put his money on Hugh Walpole. David over-praised Leslie Hartley's

Eustace and Hilda trilogy – at least I respectfully think so, notwithstanding my high opinion of the brother and sister relationship in the beginning of the first book, *The Shrimp and the Anemone*.

But his enthusiasm was surely a fault on the right side. It must have contributed to the fineness of his tuition, as it did to his friendly guidance in a private capacity. Enthusiastically he encouraged me to speak my mind, entered into my feelings, made me feel clever, and was corrective, never snubbing. When he was young, he and Anthony Asquith, nicknamed Puffin Asquith, the film director to be, were packed off by their respective parents on a sort of grand tour round the world. In the USA they had an introduction to William Randolph Hearst – Orson Welles' model for Citizen Kane – who invited them to stay in his palatial country retreat, St Simeon. David remembered a picnic there exactly like the one in the film: twenty or thirty black Rolls-Royces in convoy ferrying the guests to a small city of tents erected for the occasion. More to the point, David became friendly with Puffin's mother, Margot, wife of Prime Minister Asquith and Cynthia Asquith's step-mother-in-law, one of whose paradoxical epigrams runs: 'Genius is closely allied to sanity.' Whether or not David had a touch of genius may be an open question; but, if sanity were the test of genius, the answer would have to be affirmative.

He was sanely open-minded: he refused to discuss no polite subject whatsoever. He was usually cool and dispassionate in debate or argument, although I have heard of him getting hot under the collar and steam-rollering academic colleagues. Once he was a member of the panel of a broadcast Brains Trust, which was asked about the origins of life and the universe. The other panellists put forward scientific and atheistic explanations – astronomical, biological, mechanical and automatic. He floored them by enquiring: 'But where did the astronomy and the biology come from? Who invented the mechanism and got it going? Who invented the universe and what lies beyond it?' – and shocked their materialism by guessing that God probably created everything after all.

He was an increasingly devout Christian: another proof of his sanity in any age of faith, if not in ours. He and Rachel attended a Sunday service as a rule. Conrad Russell, a sprig of the family tree of the Dukes of Bedford and cousin of the philosopher Bertrand Russell, wrote the following tribute in a letter to a friend: 'If anyone asked what is meant by a Christian gentleman I should think of [David Cecil] as my best example. He . . . is completely charitable and uncensorious.'

Actually, there was one form of censure he resorted to: humour. Objectionable behaviour, social or literary, he would laugh to scorn, as the saying goes. Not the least of his gifts was that of ridicule: he could and did make sly, ironical, robust and always witty fun of anything which did not measure up to his standards. A typical instance of his sly wit in *Melbourne* occurs in the description of the frightful dinner party of disreputable socialites and bewildered intellectuals given by Caroline Lamb in her maddest and most perverse final phase. David wrote: 'It was not a success. Naive William Blake, it is true, was happy enough. "There is a great deal of kindness in that lady," he said, looking at Caroline.' At faults more serious

143

than naivety and silliness, David was even readier to laugh.

For that matter, Rachel was an incorrigible and reassuring laugher at catastrophe, and at whatever embarrassed or offended her. And I remember Leslie Hartley giving a devastatingly funny account of a highbrow German novel about blood-relationships: 'It's blood, blood, blood, blood from beginning to end.' And Cynthia's amusingly critical comment on *Lolita* is worthy of record. She wanted to carry on reading *Lolita* at her hairdresser's, where she was going by bus, so she removed the dust-jacket in case it should be seen and put on the dust-jacket of *Little Women*.

Interestingly, I think, Cynthia connected *Lolita* with *The Well of Loneliness*, which had come out – in more senses than one – in her youth. She was convinced that the former would be, and the latter had been, the cause of much misery. She said that *The Well of Loneliness*, the first of many 'true confessions' by a modern lesbian, might have had a liberating effect on a minority of women with the same tastes crouching in their closets, but had wrecked the lives of innumerable teachers and older women who had innocently loved younger ones and were now made to feel sexually abnormal, and, into the bad bargain, put such valuable opportunities for instruction and outlets for affection under a permanent cloud of suspicion. Her objections to *Lolita* may well be vindicated by the activities nowadays of paedophiles, child-abusers, and the sexual assaults upon, often combined with the murder of, very young girls.

David seemed to be non-political, which was strange,

considering he was descended from and related to so many eminent politicians. In his professional life he was therefore able to get on with fellow-dons and with undergraduates of most political persuasions. Yet he delivered himself of political judgments occasionally: for instance, referring to the American involvement in the strife in Vietnam, he said that no country should ever meddle in the internal affairs of another country unless it meant to govern that country – but he was not in favour of such colonisation. He also spoke comfortable words to the effect that the small size and large population of the United Kingdom, its need to trade, the loss of its empire, and the strength of its middle class, did not permit extremist politics of the right or the left to impose their drastic pseudo-solutions.

Nevertheless, in spite of his air of political detachment, of being pragmatic rather than partisan, I believe he was imbued with his family's four centuries of conservative inclinations. He wished to conserve the English monarchy, parliament and church, and many of the other evolved institutions and much of the intricate social fabric of the England he understood and loved. Above all, like the majority of us, he wanted stability, and not to have to worry about politics on top of everything else.

WOMEN ARE BETTER letter-writers than men. I generalise: but the women who have written to me do seem to have a superior aptitude and flair. Rachel's letters tended to be long, diffuse, repetitive, even gushing. They were often ungrammatical and ill-spelt. They were also extraordinarily lively and, at second glance, clever, wise and characteristic – they were like *Theresa's Choice* in having more to them than first met the eye.

A few brief excerpts from her correspondence might give a misleading impression. She wrote: 'How I agree with you about letters! I really think they oughtn't to be answered – then they can be enjoyed.' This neat aphorism is an exception to the copious rule of her style.

Yet something of her correspondence must be better than nothing, as the following excerpts will surely prove.

'David and I dined at the Zoo in London the night before last,' she wrote. 'We had a long session before dinner, walking on deserted paths, past man-made rocks, down tunnels with lit windows showing sleepy monkeys and nightmarish reptiles. I enjoyed the giraffes most. There seemed to be about eight – very elegant – weaving in and out of their stables with endless necks and mild faces, round and round, in and out, in perfect rhythm, as in a ballet.'

She described a visit to a country house: 'The dining-room was extremely noisy. With my sort of deafness, I can often hear rather better in a noisy sort of room, as people are forced to raise their voices, and the reverberations seem to help. But our hostess's soft murmur was impossible, and our host mumbled, if loudly, so I couldn't hear him either. I found myself answering at random at every meal throughout the weekend.'

Having just read *Tolstoy my Father* by Ilya Tolstoy,

146

she wrote: 'Absolutely fascinating, with far the best photographs I've seen in any book, and masses of them. It is full of vivid stories of Tolstoy, when Ilya was 10 or 12. And very appreciative of his father and understanding, yet not at all *couleur de rose* – I suppose that would be impossible for a Tolstoy.'

Rachel studied the works of Tolstoy, read everything written about him, became an expert on the subject, and did not think much of the popular biography by Henri Troyat.

At a dinner party somewhere she 'sat next to Sir A- Z-, diplomat, sometime *en poste* in Moscow, distantly related to the distinguished uncouth donnish family. I asked him if he had been to Tolstoy's house, and he replied accusingly: "Oh – you've been reading your Troyat!" Of course he thought it a very good biography. He went on to say Tolstoy was an awful bore when he got old – no good at all after *War and Peace* and *Anna Karenina*. I pointed out that although Troyat did not care about Tolstoy as a young man, and gave a very unsympathetic account of his gambling and youthful dissipations, he had not been able to help making Tolstoy's old age, and struggle to lead the life he believed in, impressive. But this led on to nothing, and Sir A- dropped the subject. I felt he had not even read "his" Troyat carefully. And I thought how well Tolstoy would have described his public face. He is rather a handsome man with a rudeness which passes for "character". He always contradicted me flat in a complacent way. I'm afraid diplomacy has a very undiplomatic effect.'

She is also afraid that she is 'becoming a Tolstoy bore

– like many women who go mad about an author. There is so much information, so much to read – one can sink oneself in the Tolstoys' family life indefinitely . . . I find Tolstoy's religious conversion extremely interesting, and the end of his life and his death moving. He became so spiritual and genuinely humble in his last year or two – I had not realised it fully. Even Countess Tolstoy admits this, though she complains bitterly and feels cut off from him. For her, the tiresome hangers-on, dropping in perpetually for meals, must have been intolerable – rather like modern hippies, without the sexual exhibitionism. I think partly why I have been so absorbed in my reading about Tolstoy is that his attitude to Christianity and God seems more possible now than it did to me in-between the wars. Or perhaps it is because I am nearer the "end of the journey".'

Her last four words in inverted commas play upon the title of my book *Memoir in the Middle of the Journey*.

Bravely risking accusations of shameless self-advertisement, but to show how lucky I was that Rachel was the friend of my work, I shall quote the continuation of the above: 'I love the last two bits of your book, *Change of Heart* and *Conclusions*. There is always hope. Generally, I don't think hope is stressed enough. People are afraid of being disappointed by wishful thinking. Yet hope is the essence of Christianity. And love is the one positive, true and absolute good when it is un-egotistic, and it makes a reason for our existence in this world. My letter is interminable, and it has turned out serious, which was not my mood when I began it. But I am so glad you've written your *Memoir* – it will get its message over to a few, in ways that you may never know, and for years and years.'

But servant problems again bring Rachel down to earth. Here she calls her Spanish couple 'nice' and 'lethargic' – the husband cannot yet have revealed his nastier un-lethargic side. 'The weather has been lovely most days, so we have gone for picnics and on expeditions – and not had a moment left over. I have enjoyed it very much, except that our daily suddenly went off on a holiday and hasn't come back when she said she would, and the nice Spanish couple *are* able to speak enough English to say they have too much to do. They are terribly lethargic, and I find myself sparing them as if they were both sixty-five instead of twenty-eight.'

And here is her account of the outbreak of hostilities between her cook Gertrude and herself – the Spaniards must have been banished in disgrace by this time: 'Our daily went away for Christmas and then, poor thing, developed two agonising abscesses in her front teeth and, as no dentist was working, had to have them torn out without an anaesthetic by a doctor. She has only been able to come back today – quite recovered – and at last after a fortnight the house is being cleaned. As a result of her absence, Gertrude became quite unlike herself, suddenly very much a martyr and slightly menacing about us "having so many visitors". Laura and I were reduced to washing up glasses in the bathroom secretly – with many breakages in the washbasin, needless to say . . . Now that David and I are alone again, Gertrude is as nice as can be. However, it was disillusioning, the Jekyll and Hyde atmosphere. I had thought that worrying about servants was a thing of the past. Anyhow it is preferable to worrying about one's children. But I fear that cooks with strong characters always win.'

Relations with Gertrude had clearly gone from bad to worse when Rachel wrote: 'Gertrude is off on her fortnight's holiday to the Isle of Skye on a bus. She has locked up her flat in a misanthropic way, so that the temporary cook can't sit in it, and tacked three days onto the fortnight to recover from the bus-ride. No doubt she will need them. Perhaps she and her fellow-sightseers will all be driven over the edge of a cliff, like so many pensioners on their holidays.'

Yet the alternative to a professional in the kitchen did not appeal. 'I am better,' Rachel wrote, 'but last night at dinner with a neighbour ate a delicious but over-rich meal cooked by her and had a very bad night – so did David. Amateur cooks are fatal.'

The Cecils and I shared three figurative means of describing personality and mood to our own satisfaction: we had the specification of leprechaun, we estimated the number of mental events that might occur to someone in a period of time, and we guessed at the physical state of the lower part of the large intestine, called the colon, by way of a psychological guide.

Thus, we had mutual friends with unexcited colons, feeble colons, nervous colons, whiplash colons, and so on.

The consequences of Gertrude's behaviour for Rachel were 'rigid colon nights'.

SHE WROTE: 'I do find now that a siesta is of vital importance. I am depressed by how much less I get through during the day. The odd thing is that one's children take up more time emotionally when grown up. I can't be detached. I suppose they might like it better if I were, and wasn't always trying to "save" them.'

Then she was 'half in bed after a violent throat infection and high temperature for a week. I should like always to get up for breakfast every day, and then go back to bed, and to reading and writing, until lunchtime. I'm sure I could get on with another novel if I did this. But somehow one is like a bit of straw that blows about – I do duties and shop and waste time in the mornings. And I see I am beginning to ramble weakly. I haven't been ill for two years, and it is like a new sensation, the extreme weakness on first getting up. Also, I was taken aback on glancing in the bathroom looking-glass. Instead of the transparent purified look after flu that one used to have when younger, I saw a little wizened old woman with hollow yet bunged-up eyes, lips like a piece of string and hair like a cheap wig. The only compensation is that I am in excellent spirits. Moreover Mima [Lady Harlech, her elder sister-in-law] is staying here. She says that now, aged eighty, she doesn't feel things as much as she did – one mercy of old age.'

Rachel described a friend of hers, a leprechaun, recently widowed, who did not find it merciful: 'F. is grief-stricken, utterly, like a child. She wants to die more than anything. She has nothing to live for now that he has died – he was her whole life and support and pleasure. What is pathetic is that she has no mature power of dealing with grief – is not "glad for his sake" – has no pretences – and no thought of the effect her grief might have on others . . . I really can't feel that suicide is so very wrong.'

The trend of Rachel's thoughts was no doubt darkened by the death of Bobbety round about now. 'Poor poor Betty! And David feels it very much,' she wrote as unselfishly as usual.

But her spirits revived, although she was recuperating from another illness.

'Having just discovered that my electric typewriter works perfectly on a bed-tray, I have felt a sudden impulse to write to you – but on condition that you don't answer. David went off to Bobbety's Memorial Service yesterday. He said it was very splendid and appropriate – four Prime Ministers present and the Archbishop of Canterbury – the latter in dishevelled surplice and billowing lawn sleeves looking, in Bobbety's own phrase, "like an unmade bed". I am still weak, but seem to be euphoric.'

She was sufficiently euphoric to indulge in almost black humour: 'I have given up sleeping pills after taking the smallest possible dose of Seconal every night for the last ten years. It doesn't make much difference. I sleep only slightly worse, and think about death in the mornings now instead of in the evenings.'

But distressing evidence of the depredations of time was hardly to be avoided any more.

'We came here to Derbyshire with Mima to stay with Moucher. Old age has great sadness. Mima, who had more feeling than anyone, and was wonderfully strengthening to be with, and so funny, is now 87 and almost stone deaf. It makes her frustrated and bored. I think the effort of living fills up her days exclusively. Still, we have had a great deal of talk and laughter.'

And again: 'I confess I feel rather stunned by all the entertaining over Christmas . . . The C-Ls and some other people came here for drinks.' The C-Ls, Bob and Mary, were elderly literary neighbours. Bob C-L was for ever fighting his alcoholism, and Mary was understandably low-toned. Rachel continued: 'Mary became quite animated and uncharacteristically kicked over her full tumbler of gin and tonic on the carpet. Poor Bob had obviously taken his pill, so refused even lime juice. He looked older than ever, with his beard a few inches longer. He has given up smoking too, so he seems half the man he was.'

My personal situation underwent a sea-change, I was freer emotionally, and confided in Rachel, who wrote in various letters: 'I think one should always "explore" – it does not necessarily do any harm – and if the miracle occurred you might find someone who would make you very happy . . . After all, the loneliness is so sad later on for the unmarried, and I'm sure you were never meant to be single . . . I am not racking my brains for possible wives for you, and hope you won't think so. I was just pleased when you told me you were ready to contemplate the idea . . . And now that the door is open I feel something may turn up, romance or marriage, which would give you a new lease of life – not that you need one – that sounds very patronising – but it is exciting to consider the infinite possibilities before you.'

Her three children married and in the natural course of things she wrote to me: 'I have been *completely* occupied with looking after my baby grandson since last Monday. He is lying asleep in his carrycot behind the sofa in the drawing-room at the moment, and I am sitting peacefully by a blazing fire – by great luck we have not had anyone to stay since last Saturday. It is strangely exhausting, but also satisfying. He is such an engaging little baby, and very responsive. He reminds me of Hugh [he was Hugh and Mirabel's son]. He is pale with lovely little hands, a humorous crooked smile, and appears forward for his age.'

FAREWELL

ONE WEEKEND, WHEN I was staying at Red Lion House, a crisis in the kitchen was allowed to impinge upon the sociability. Gertrude had walked out at short notice, or a temporary cook had been more temporary than intended, and Rachel had to feed us. She hardly knew how to boil an egg, as they say; and she compounded the problem of her ignorance by refusing to interrupt or cut short conversations in the sitting-room, or change the routine of our enjoyment. Thus, at about eight o'clock in the evening, when we might have been eating dinner, she would begin to think of preparing it. Then she would be shocked by the work involved, flustered by the time it took to stew a chicken, say, and embarrassed by the unappetising appearance and taste of the meal she eventually served. She loathed the whole business. Politeness notwithstanding, she showed that she could summon no enthusiasm for the task – on the contrary. It was probably some relief that David did not interfere, or hinder her by trying to help, or care what or when or even if he ate, and was so uncomplaining. On the other hand she might have longed at moments for a husband who would and could do the necessary.

That cook-less period was protracted, and I believe

Rachel gave up the unequal struggle to the extent that she and David almost lived on water-biscuits for several months, and their health suffered in consequence.

But the weekend of their evident discomfiture, partly caused by concerned and erroneous assumptions in respect of my discomfort, was exceptional. As a rule they rose above trial and tribulation for the sake of their friends: at least every other meeting I can recall was marked by their happy poise and outgoing interest in life in general and my life in particular.

The sentence above is that much more of a compliment because they were both highly-strung types. Rachel at some stage of her girlhood had eaten compulsively – she told amusing tales of devouring the contents of the fridge. David, like Edward Clare in *Theresa's Choice*, had been a hypochondriac – he said the cure for hypochondria was marriage. They did not grow out of, and they found no cure for, worrying about their children. They were all too aware of having given hostages to fortune; and Rachel wished in vain that she could be maternally more detached, and David was apologetic, for instance on account of his fearful agitation when Jonathan, Hugh and Laura were young and late home from the Dragon School.

Yet the Cecils never unloaded even the cares of parenthood on outsiders.

In passing I would just add that, although excesses of parental devotion may have a restrictive effect on the liberty of youth, their children now, safely wed and successful, seem only to have benefited from having been loved so much.

Far from complaining of any of the cares of matrimony,

David and Rachel preached its advantages, especially to me as soon as they thought I was in a receptive frame of mind. On weekend walks, perhaps around the verges of farmed fields on the slopes of Cranborne Chase, or along the cart-track in the shallow valley below Cranborne Manor, he would halt abruptly to emphasise the point that his temporary fears of marriage were converted into permanent joys once the deed was done. I see again his pale complexion, rectangular brow, grey eyes, small and kindly, crooked nose, and again hear his oddly modulated rush of words. He would expatiate upon the simplifying warmth of Rachel's affection and the endlessly intriguing complexity of her intelligence. He would marvel at her unselfishness and say she was the making of him and hope that I might be as lucky as he had been.

And Rachel in her turn, walking briskly beside me, a slim, still girlish figure, her brown hair showing hardly any grey, would reiterate with diffident conviction, and by way of a warning against the wrong partner, having again described her marriage to the right one, that egotism was not very nice to live with. But her smile and nod – her smiling eyes under high, slightly bristling, surprised eyebrows – were encouraging.

Miraculously, the more so because not long after the Cecils ventured to express interest in my romantic destiny, I met and married my wife.

They did not know her. No doubt they wished to like and be liked by her. They had reached the age which metaphor has called 'the front line': too many old comrades and boon companions had fallen or were falling in the existential battle. Rachel's elder brother died, and

David was suddenly and to all intents and purposes the surviving member of his generation of the Cecil family, for Mima as well as Bobbety was dead, and Moucher had retreated into her long last illness and beyond his reach. And Leslie Hartley and Puffin Asquith were no more. Naturally they would have been keener to gain another 'best' friend, rather than to lose one.

I was equally keen not to let my marriage come between us. More positively I was proud of Gilly, wanted to show her off, and give David and Rachel the pleasure of her company – and vice versa.

They trundled up to London to have dinner with us. The keynote of the occasion was instant and mutual approval. Then, on another evening, we went together to a performance of *The Magic Flute*. David had been taken to the opera when he was a boy, and thrilled by the scene of *Mountains and Two Armed Men*. The men in armour sing that whoever can conquer the fear of death will be released from worldly bondage and ascend from earth towards heaven. Precocious as David surely was in boyhood, I attribute his thrill less to sage words in German and more to the gripping visual imagery and the aural delight. Again, sixty-odd years later on, he was moved by the same scene and – as always – by Mozart's music. And during the opera he blessed my marriage by saying that he felt it was and would be as happy as his own.

WE STAYED WITH the Cecils, and met them again when we were staying with the Trees. Of course, looking back, we did not see them often enough, perhaps two or three times a year. Gilly was dazzled by David and loved him, and she and Rachel became firm friends. Sometimes David and I spoke on the telephone – companionable hour-long conversations, terminated regretfully at my end of the line.

I did not notice that they were growing older. Rachel seemed to be immune from the ageing process, and David was as spry, talkative, quick-witted and jolly as ever. And they willingly turned out on winter evenings to drive the fifteen miles from Cranborne to Donhead St Mary to dine with Anne and Michael Tree.

Setting aside the facts that David was Anne's uncle and she was his niece, also the motive and the magnetism of affection, the Cecils were still gregarious. True, they tried a little harder to space out their social engagements; yet they continued to enjoy gatherings of like-minded people. After all, socially speaking, he was a star performer in need of an audience; and he and she possessed in abundance the quality that keeps the wheels of society turning – curiosity.

In this context, in some puritanical quarters, David was regarded as a victim of his success. Earnest souls, who were not entreated by irresistible hostesses to come and entertain the world of fashion, who were untroubled by tempting invitations to flutter round lit candles, were inclined to think he was too sociable by half; that he scattered his pearls before swine, and squandered time and talent that might have been put to better use, studying and writing learned disquisitions.

But David was nothing if not balanced. My rebuttal of the criticism above would be, first, that his life was by no means bounded by books, and, secondly, that another distinctive feature of his writing was the width of the experience and the breadth of the sympathy that informed it. He wrote so much the better for having inside information about aristocrats and meritocrats, rulers as well as ruled, stately homes and the groves of academe, town and country – as a young man he had explored London, living in his family's house in Arlington Street. Although he was born a grandee, he could understand and feel for Charles Lamb, who was the son of a liveried servant.

He had recently set to work on his *Portrait of Charles Lamb*. The years of his retirement had been prolific: he had published *The Cecils of Hatfield House*; his fine anthology with the unfortunate title *Library Looking-Glass*; and *A Portrait of Jane Austen*, the elusive subject of which he managed to bring amazingly to life.

For ages he had wanted to write about his beloved Jane Austen, and he may have felt that the book represented some sort of completion of his literary career. Certainly, after it, he was rather at a loose end, wondering what to do next. He greatly admired that hero of literature and life, Sir Walter Scott, but realised he was no longer equal to the task either of a critique of all the Waverley Novels, or a full biography. He therefore settled on telling the story of Charles Lamb, which was shorter; terribly dramatic, since Charles' sister Mary went mad and murdered their mother; and inspiringly altruistic in that Charles aged twenty-one dedicated the rest of his days to looking after Mary. Moreover David had an old soft spot for the quirky literary genius of Lamb.

He must have written his books with a certain facility. Notwithstanding various interruptions of his work in progress, to fulfil family obligations, teach, review others' books for newspapers, broadcast, meet friends, go to parties, travel and so on, he never seemed to lose his thread or get stuck. He voiced none of the traditional grouses of Grub Street, for instance that literary composition was hell on earth and publishers were the very devil.

I can remember him showing no sign of the strain of authorship in his own home – Germ Q was a different matter; and in the happy ambience of Anne and Michael's he communicated an even stronger impression of not having a care in the world. He could and would hold the table, and in the drawing-room after dinner he was apt to spring to his feet and stand in front of the fire and engage in even more animated conversation, or interject some ironical remark, tongue in cheek, or enthuse about a book or dissect a character or be killingly funny, just as he had long ago when I made his acquaintance at Compton Place.

Meanwhile Rachel's lack of egotism displayed another sort of brilliance. She never competed with David, she was not resentful of his success, she did not try to put spokes in his flying wheels. Thus she maintained her dignity and her modest yet stalwart individuality. She seemed as pleased as the rest of us were to listen to her husband, to continue to listen to him after forty years, and to laugh at his jokes. Her own conversational contributions were unforced and pointful.

But a shadow now falls across my memories of the Cecils.

One Saturday evening at dinner at the Trees', Rachel, who was sitting next to me, said that she had had everything a heart could desire, done everything, seen everything, so was no longer afraid of death, in fact would not mind dying too much.

She spoke lightly – she was not going against the festive grain of the occasion. Her sentiments carried a stage further our perennial discussion of the mysteries of death – and my writing's preoccupation with bearing and surviving it.

I was interested, but not startled. Perhaps I did not – could not at a dinner party – pay proper attention. We soon changed the subject.

Some time later, on a walk at Cranborne, she reverted to it. She said she was so fulfilled by life, as wife, mother and in every other way, that, although she hoped not to abandon David and would be very worried about him if she had to, also hated to think of parting from her children, she herself was now ready or readier to die in not too disagreeable a fashion. She was not at all gloomy – why should she have been gloomy? She had almost become the character in the song of Mozart's *Armed*

Men: she was conquering the fear of death and *en route*, metaphorically, for heaven.

Besides, she was fit and well – she was assuming an attitude to an event that was merely hypothetical – not that her courage was ever in doubt.

There may have been a connection between these two declarations of hers and then her illness.

A LAYMAN'S EUPHEMISTIC description of it could be: defeat in her lifelong battle against tiredness.

The spiritual challenge issued by serious ill-health, or one of the challenges, takes the form of disappointment: how do we deal with, how are we to put up with, the dashing of one hope of recovery after another?

At first Rachel reported to me that she felt weak. The doctors, as usual, attributed her weakness to a virus. But their prescriptions that were going to cure her failed to do so. And she felt weaker. Her own ideas of what was wrong with her, and what would rectify the trouble, proved erroneous. The disappointments multiplied; she bore them with almost misleading equanimity. Eventually she went into hospital for tests.

I cannot remember the exact sequence of events. At some stage David was told that she would not recover. He had not thought of it, he had not dared to, was stunned, did not know if he could bear it, or how, for once, to deceive Rachel – he believed for several weeks or even months that she was unaware of the mortal nature of her illness. She came home, and strange to relate, incredibly maybe, they resumed life together on lines not too far removed from normality – he continued to write *Charles Lamb*, and she was again supportive and cheerful, although she did have to spend more time in bed.

But in fact she had realised she was dying either during or before her spell in hospital – she had written to her confidential friend Margaret Ricketts about her impending fate. She rose to the challenge of the ultimate disappointment, she kept death at bay verbally, to 'save' her husband and children for as long as she could, according to her habit. Her success, her gallantry, caused one of those unintended ill-effects of good intentions: temporarily and unwontedly she had to keep her secret from them, and they had to try to keep the same secret from her.

Yet soon enough they all reached an understanding, the tacit and probably the best kind of understanding, I gather. In these circumstances, what is to be said that will not make everything worse, apart from practical questions asked and answered with love?

We still corresponded. 'A packet of my school letters, written between the ages of 10 and 11 from the Convent des Oiseaux, has been discovered,' she informed me. 'I was very interested to read them. Lots of things I remember vividly, but I had quite forgotten how anxious I was to do well in my lessons and especially in the exams, though my mother, while praising me, was not particularly interested.'

Obliquely she referred to her mother again: 'My home-sick pleadings must have been hard to withstand.'

I sent her a copy of Philip Toynbee's *Part of a Journey*. She had known the author, who had just died, and other members of his family. She had not only done and seen everything, but known everybody who was anybody in the artistic establishment for half a century and more, first as the daughter of her parents, then in her own right, also because she was the wife of David, and thanks to her connection with the university. I was often taken aback by the Cecils' assured assessments of the intellectual ability of younger persons who were trying to climb the greasy pole of reputation. Their assurance was based upon David having either taught, or examined for the award of degrees or prizes, such persons, and on similar judgments passed along the university grapevine. Thus, for instance, when Ken Tynan was at the height of his powers as arbiter of all matters theatrical, David mentioned the silly statements he had made for effect during some viva.

Rachel was critical of Toynbee's book, its depressing aspects, but 'enthralled' by it. The following generalis-ation is an offshoot of her criticism: 'What is so sad, looking back at life, is that most people are more attrac-tive when they are young. Their spirits are so much higher.'

I rang up Red Lion House for news of her health and, latterly, to support or to divert David. Although she hated talking on the telephone, she did so at least once, she may even have rung me on her return from the testing time in hospital. She wanted to tell me her illness was

165

temporary. 'The doctors are certain it'll be temporary, which is a relief.' I took the hint and rightly or wrongly, but mainly because I was rendered somewhat speechless by her confirmation of my worst fears, did not comment on it.

Her intention must have been to tell me the truth and to ask me to help her to take no notice, keep up appearances, rise above it. She wrote: 'I do hope you are both well. I am rather doddery today, otherwise quite well.'

Again: 'Laura is expecting her baby from today. I do wish I was stronger and could help more, as I was able to with Leo.'

Gilly and I stayed with the Trees and drove over to see Rachel one morning. She had dressed and she came downstairs to chat to us for half an hour. She was slightly thinner and paler, yet managed to seem unchanged.

However she wrote a sort of goodbye: 'You have been so wonderfully faithful and such a good and cheering friend with your letters and pcs.'

Her illness gained ground: 'I feel rather drowsy, and my mouth tastes like very hot curry and mustard.'

Then she wrote: 'Most of the day I am like a non-arthritic woman of ninety – not "wonderful for her years" – and I simply have to collapse on my bed with a book. It is such a blessing that I can completely absorb myself . . . The great thing is to live for the moment . . . The children have been marvellous.'

She died in 1982, having been born in 1909.

At her funeral the prayer composed by Jane Austen was read: 'Heavenly Father, look with compassion upon

166

the afflicted of every condition, assuage the pangs of disease, comfort the broken in spirit.'

IN REPLY TO my letter of condolence, David wrote of her 'goodness and sweetness and humour, but also her unbounded curiosity about life and people, and the idealism with which she judged them. It was this, of course, that accounted for her special interest in Tolstoy, man as well as writer . . . It was this, too, which made the last year of her life so extraordinary. She realised before me, though I did not know it, that she was dying of cancer, and faced and accepted the fact absolutely fearlessly – and was able to make me and the children accept it too, if not quite as she did. I said to Hugh a few days ago, "You have been a great support throughout." "No," he answered, "Mama supported us all." I am afraid she did feel very wretched in the end, but she suffered no acute pain. She did not complain – was always herself though growingly weak – and died peacefully in her sleep lying beside me. I should not be pitied too much yet. After the first shock nearly a year ago, which was shattering, I seem to have been like someone under a local anaesthetic, knowing what was happening to me but not really feeling it . . . I suppose I have not yet taken in the fact of her death, and I simply don't believe the parting is for ever.'

Some of our pity, which was irrepressible, was reserved for the practical side of David's future. He had been dependent on Rachel in so many areas. An extreme example of his dependence was provided by the electric blanket they slept under, the double-bed sort, but controlled by a single switch. I told Rachel that modern electric blankets for two had a pair of switches; but she was afraid that David would soon be in trouble if he got his hands on a switch of his own. What happened at night at present, she said, was safer and simpler: he might wake up and mumble 'Too cold!' or 'Too hot!' – whereupon she adjusted the temperature of the blanket.

Who would adjust it now? Who would cook him a bite to eat?

But his children were as 'marvellous' to their father as they had been to their mother. They took over Rachel's managerial duties and found him a competent and kind housekeeper. And he himself coped better than expected – he arranged to be driven out and about by a friendly taxi-driver. That he took the minimum of interest in what he ate, if he ate, and in other homely matters, must have made him easier to look after.

Moreover his children visited and kept him company. He had added in a postscript to the letter already quoted: 'I am always here, except for the odd day or two away.' He did stay put at Red Lion House for some time after Rachel's illness and death: he was aware of the traditional wisdom which warns that if you leave your home immediately after suffering a horrible experience in it, you will never be able to return. But slowly he began to supply the demands of all the people queueing up to entertain him.

Part of the point of that postscript was to suggest he

was ready to be visited. He also wrote, and said repeatedly on the telephone: 'Please let us meet soon.' Yet several best-laid schemes, for us to stay with him and vice versa, went wrong because he cancelled them: he was sorry, he had got in a muddle, he would be elsewhere, or there was something he could not wriggle out of doing. At length it occurred to us that he was not only – and thankfully – leading a busier social life, but that he was reluctant to revive the happy and unhappy memories of our former foursome. Besides, it would have been a strain for him to be our host without the customary hostess; and he did not know Gilly as well as he knew me, and so on. We fully understood, and sympathised with, such feelings.

We all met nonetheless on neutral ground, at Anne and Michael's, for instance, and he and I maintained telephonic communication.

He raised the technique of talking on the telephone to the status of an art-form. He was natural and spontaneous – he caused many costly minutes to pass in a flash. He answered the telephone in a low and unapprehensive voice, and when he rang me up he would declare his whole name – 'It's David Cecil' – although he sounded like no other David. Science and distance between them seemed to concentrate the charm of his conversation.

We spoke mostly of Rachel. He wished to – but his wish was by no means unilateral. He was haunted by the memory of being told that her illness was terminal: the nastiest side-effect of his sorrow had been the conviction that he was going to let her, his children and himself down. Yet he was proved wrong, he did not collapse. The fortitude he said he had been lent, and the unwavering heroism she had shown, combined to corroborate his view of the sweet mystery and miraculousness of life, and to reinforce his religious faith. He had been holding her hand when she died.

I wrote to him after reading *Charles Lamb*, and he wrote back: 'Though he is not a kindred spirit in the way Jane Austen is . . . I did become devoted to him and awed by the beauty of his character . . . Writing it in my particular circumstances was not so remarkable. I had written two thirds before I knew about Rachel's illness and the last third was already planned.'

Even if the artist's panacea is to practise his or her art, I disagree with David's modest disclaimer and continue to think it extremely remarkable that he finished the book.

I imagine that Lamb's capacity for self-denying love was a subject more suited to his frame of mind in the relevant period than Melbourne's worldliness would have been.

David asked if he might borrow and read the letters Rachel had written me, and explained when he returned them: 'I often looked at one in order as it were to hear her voice again.'

In another sense, I guess, he heard her voice increasingly clearly. He believed in resurrection, as indeed she had; and he talked more and more often of life after death, although, like the majority of very intelligent people who have shared his beliefs, he never described the form he expected it to take or made too much of the possibility of reunion with loved ones. The gradual transference of his attention to the next world was an object lesson in the benefit and blessing of religion.

NOT THAT DAVID ever lost interest in this world. He kept his promise to Rachel to write a biographical Introduction to his selection of her father's work, *Desmond MacCarthy, The Man and his Writings*. He researched and produced his guide to the manor houses of Dorset, and selected and introduced *A Choice of Bridges's Verse*.

His grief was not inward-looking – he was not self-centred. When my mother died he wrote to me as follows: 'I never knew her to talk to, I wish I had. But she is a very well-remembered figure from my young days – the perfect image of elegance and distinction – I remember her particularly at a ball in a lovely dress with spreading skirts of pale pink and lilac petals – her fair head and exquisitely alive intelligent countenance. Her death cannot have come as a surprise to you . . . But the loss of a parent is inevitably strange and sad.'

In these latter years he was no less appreciative of beauty in all its forms. He had loved especially – aesthetically, I mean – three women noted for their physical beauty, Cynthia Asquith, Diana Cooper, and Joan Drogheda to whom he dedicated *Max*. He also loved that trio for their equally outstanding qualities of mind and spirit, and referred repeatedly to the common fallacy which suggests that plain women are nicer than pretty ones. He had always been alarmed and repelled by houris, semi-professional *femmes fatales*, sex-kittens, and even more so by hungry sex-cats. He seemed to think it was the first duty of femininity to exercise its innate genius for making men better than they otherwise would be – so to sympathise, so to frown and smile, as to make them happier, more sensitive, kinder and gentler.

Let me hasten to add, before feminism red in tooth and claw pounces on the sentence above, that David gave at least as good as he hoped to get from women: the secret of his charm was that everyone susceptible to it felt cleverer, more cultivated, more reasonable and cheerful, after meeting and talking to him.

He still talked fast and with enviable fluency, although not out of turn. Here is a trio of his epigrammatic funny phrases: he was amused by 'the shamelessness of the psycho-analysed'; he described a handsome dull historian of our acquaintance as looking like 'a trivial eagle'; and from the television programme Come Dancing he drew the following conclusion: 'I can't believe there's much wrong with this country when I watch Come Dancing.'

But in spite of the attentiveness of his family and friends, and writing and reading books, and the telephone and television, he grew lonelier. He missed Rachel, and confessed that he sometimes felt cross with her for not being there to share his every experience and to let him share hers. He wrote: 'I can't agree with you about my being the perfect widower. I am all right when talking to someone like you, but alone I often get gloomy and, what is worse, fussy about unimportant matters. I have to remind myself how lucky I have been to have had fifty years of a marriage as happy as any I could have dreamed of.'

His health began to fail in a way almost symbolic: he developed heart trouble. He told me it was not too unpleasant and, more than anything else, made him feel tired. Perhaps in order not to worry me, he conveyed an impression that it was something of a relief to him to retire to bed – matrimony had certainly done wonders for his hypochondria! But I would not wish to belittle his courage or, thanks to religion, his confidence in the future.

He also trusted his doctor. He and Rachel formed a friendship with Dr Ian Geddes during her illness, and had been deeply grateful for his ministrations, including the visits, which he arranged, by a nurse trained to comfort people in their situation.

David's appreciation of the helpfulness of this Macmillan nurse struck me as touchingly characteristic. He was cleverer than anybody, he seemed to me to understand everything, yet he was humble enough to learn new lessons from a stranger. And his humanity valued and was reinforced by her vocational compassion, and as one thoroughgoing professional he was prepared to recognise the authority of another.

But now he, like Rachel before him, was moving out of reach of medicine, except in a palliative sense. I went to stay with Anne and Michael, and drove across to spend an hour or so with him. He was upstairs in the big double bed in his and Rachel's bedroom at the top of the stairs: it looked over the garden and the garden wall at the field in which the Cornish elms had flanked the old drive to Cranborne Manor, and the quiet Dorset countryside beyond. He was composed and welcoming, and wore a tattered jersey on top of his pyjamas.

Once more we spoke of Rachel. He reverted, either on this occasion or in the course of another conversation round about this time, to the period of his courtship. He told me in a tone of undimmed admiration that Rachel had written him a letter similar to that which Theresa writes to Edward Clare in her novel. He thought it brave and brilliant of her to have done so, and that almost entirely to it they owed their marriage, their children and all their happiness. For he had hesitated on the brink of the matrimonial abyss, he explained: he was not in his first impulsive youth, he was far from sure he would be a good husband, he dreaded the possible disillusion and discontent of a wife. He had therefore belatedly – though perhaps better late than never – drawn back. But then Rachel had taken the unconventional and positively forward step of writing to release him from emotional obligation and to sue for the continuation of their friendship. She subtly and gracefully renounced his love which he had not dared to declare. He was thus contrarily set free both to love her and to propose to her.

He read a whole liberal education into that epistle of hers. He claimed that he had gained a rule of life from it as well as a wife, since she had succeeded by coming to terms with failure, and won by resigning herself to loss.

Soon after my visit his health deteriorated. Jonathan went to be with him at Red Lion House. I understand that at the end he said to Jonathan: 'I'd like to go to sleep now,' and turned his head on the pillow and died.

It was the first of January 1986. He was eighty-four years old.

ONE MORE WORD, ladies and gentlemen, and I shall have finished – as verbose public speakers are apt falsely to promise.

These memories of mine may seem to be too much *couleur de rose*. That critical idiom sometimes employed by Rachel could be applied to them, I suppose.

But I would rather not speak ill of the dead, let alone write it about these four 'best' friends either of mine or of one another, whom I admired, and have many reasons to be grateful to.

Besides, I hardly knew Leslie Hartley well enough to dish the reconstituted dirt – if any – in the approved modern mode. I remember him almost exclusively at Cynthia Asquith's dining-room table, a bald burly middle-aged man bearing a certain resemblance to a seal and looking comfortable, smiling and talking expressively and being indescribably droll and radiating goodwill. His eyes were like blue windows into his receptive wondering artist's soul, and he had long-fingered artist's hands, too.

Again, I did not know Cynthia in her youth and beauty, or in a family setting, or indeed for long. Nevertheless I would not like to be less dependable than she was, and less loyal to her than she would have been to me. How could I, why should I, castigate her for apparently being a model daughter, a responsible wife, a mother bravely doing her best in tragic circumstances, for writing several first-rate books and always having cohorts of friends, and for her goodness to myself?

No doubt her manner was too abrupt, her opinions too trenchant, her politics too pragmatic, and her class too upper to suit everyone. Her inclination to react against, to challenge and to mock dogma, pomposity and fashionable idols and shibboleths must have made enemies. Her beauty and her brains, her powerful sense of the ridiculous and the detachment of her superiority, were bound to have been held against her in some quarters.

Yet personally, and from various literary points of view, I continue to miss, as the Cecils did, not what others might call her failings but what we called her uniqueness. To put it more simply, we were sorry she was no longer with us exactly as she had been, unchanged, and we grieved that she was irreplaceable.

Once, long ago, Rachel told me flatly that she did not like a book of mine, which shall be nameless. Her uncompromising attitude shocked me. But I came round to thinking she was at least partially right. Later on I realised that, in the sort of awkward situation in which she found herself, honesty has to be the best policy. Finally, of course, her dislike of one book added to the value of her liking of the others.

From this episode I deduced, or maybe it provided corroboration, that she was so direct and idealistic as to be potentially formidable.

Moreover I can dredge up a few negatives that may help to describe her: like Theresa, she was born to be nothing but a wife and mother, not a spinster or mistress or career-girl; she was less sensual than affectionate, and less temperamental than steadily sensitive; she was neither the ambitious bullying type of hostess, thanks be, nor a clothes-horse nor a fashion-plate; she was not at all wicked, or even bad, or dotty, or sloppy; and she did not wear her charm and wisdom on her sleeve.

The pair of negatives applicable to David that occur to me are: he was more aesthete, and more Johnny-head-in-air, than smart man of the world, although he understood very well how the world worked; and he distrusted passion, he had rather a blind spot about physical passion, and not too much sympathy with irrational obsessive feelings. If his beloved Jane Austen had written about him, the book might have been an intriguing study of contrasts entitled *Sentiment and Sentimentality*. He was chock-full of sentiment, but had no time and not much patience with sentimentality. He advised me not to visit a friend who was mentally ill and unlikely to recognise me. He himself was temporarily loth to visit his sister Moucher when she was in the same sad state as my friend: he thought their encounter, at best, would be merely and mutually harrowing, and would blot out his memory of the sentient person he loved.

Isaiah Berlin wrote an obituary of David for the Royal Society of Literature, and ended it thus: 'He was certainly the most delightful human being that anyone could ever hope to meet.'

He was the youngest child of his parents, lovable and much loved. He proved that a good son to his mother can make a good husband. He was even too caring a father: is that possible? He excelled as writer and teacher, and was at least a great friend to a great many people. His life was really a work of art by his own standards, in that he introduced delight into every expression of it.

Isaiah Berlin's positive epithet would describe the whole of my friendship both with David and with Rachel. My memories are exclusively of the differing delights of having known each of them, and the delightful atmosphere they created together.

INDEX